KU-545-756

'Hers is an escape story from the working-class home . . . As she speeds towards independence, we are gagged, bound and bundled into the back of her getaway car, unable to do anything but gawp at her daring' *Sunday Times*

'Janet is her own finest creation . . . What is overwhelming is her seething, irrepressible hunger for life' *Observer*

'An extraordinary tale of ferocious ambition and the lengths to which one had to be prepared to go in order to clamber a little way up the greasy pole of the English class system' London's *Evening Standard*

'It will confirm her enemies' prejudices and make no new friends. How very refreshing!' *Independent*

'*Baggage* is fast, furious, belligerent' *Guardian Weekend*

'Flamboyant, outspoken, charismatic . . . Janet Street-Porter has written a brilliant and unflinchingly frank account of her childhood and teenage years' *Daily Mail*

Janet Street-Porter moved from the *Daily Mail* to the London *Evening Standard*, and from broadcasting on LBC Radio in the 1970s to presenting, devising and producing shows for London Weekend Television. From 1988 to 1994 she was BBC Head of Youth and Entertainment Features, winning a BAFTA for originality in 1988. She spent a brief period as managing director of cable channel L!ive TV, was made editor of the *Independent on Sunday* in 1999 and is now an Editor at Large for the *Independent*.

BAGGAGE
My Childhood

Janet Street-Porter

headline

For Pat

Thanks to: The Sisterhood

Copyright © 2004 Janet Street-Porter

All photographs belong to the author or her sister.

The right of Janet Street-Porter to be identified as the Author of
the Work has been asserted by her in accordance with the
Copyright, Designs and Patents Act 1988.

First published in 2004
by HEADLINE BOOK PUBLISHING

First published in paperback in 2005
by HEADLINE BOOK PUBLISHING

10 9 8 7 6 5 4 3

Apart from any use permitted under UK copyright law, this publication
may only be reproduced, stored, or transmitted, in any form,
or by any means, with prior permission in writing of the publishers or,
in the case of reprographic production, in accordance with the terms
of licences issued by the Copyright Licensing Agency.

Every effort has been made to fulfil requirements with regard to
reproducing copyright material. The author and publisher will be glad to
rectify any omissions at the earliest opportunity.

Suburbia
Words and music by Neil Tennant and Chris Lowe
© 1986 Cage Music Limited. Sony Publishing Limited ATV Music
All rights reserved.

Cataloguing in Publication Data is available from the British Library

ISBN 0 7553 1266 X

Typeset in Perpetua by Avon DataSet Ltd, Bidford-on-Avon, Warwickshire

Printed and bound in Great Britain by
Mackays of Chatham plc, Chatham, Kent

Headline's policy is to use papers that are natural, renewable and
recyclable products and made from wood grown in sustainable forests.
The logging and manufacturing processes are expected to conform to
the environmental regulations of the country of origin.

HEADLINE BOOK PUBLISHING
A division of Hodder Headline
338 Euston Road, London NW1 3BH

www.headline.co.uk
www.hodderheadline.com

Contents

Prologue

She stares back at me, sulky, suspicious, distrustful, holding my gaze. There isn't a day when she's not here, shadowing me from the minute I wake up. In the bathroom, in the reflection of a shop window when I go to buy newspapers. At the hairdressers when I look up from a magazine. Whenever I try on a dress, she watches the proceedings with slightly pursed lips and a disapproving expression. I rip off the offending garment and rush from the store. Too fat, too old, trying to look fashionable, mutton dressed as lamb. That's what she would be thinking. Why won't she leave me alone? She's here now while I write this, staring back at me from the train window, daring me to carry on.

At what point in my life did I start to morph into the

person I loathe? What crime or misdemeanour did I commit to trigger off the process? Why can't I look like those laughing happy photos of me as a student in the 1960s, but gracefully older? Why am I turning inexorably into her – the saggy chin, the baggy eyes, the sour expression? For, if your face is a product of your life, mine has been so very different to hers. I have been well educated, well travelled, well read. I've soaked up contemporary culture, been assiduously open to new ideas, nurtured a wide circle of friends. I don't smoke, I don't speak Welsh, I don't have roots in a small coastal village on the edge of the mountains. I've been careful with myself, spending a fortune on face cream, building a gym in my house, hiring the services of a personal trainer. I live in architect-designed spaciousness with modern art on the walls, everything hidden away, not a fancy plate to be dusted or today's *Daily Mail* lying open on the table at the Coffee Break page. My house represents everything I am. But she's living in it.

This gradual transformation is driving me mad. Not a day passes without active consideration of cosmetic surgery, analysis, medication. I want to stop the process before it goes any further. I don't want to end up like she did, bitter, lonely, petty and pitied by everyone who came into contact with her. She's probably reading this and gloating. She's finally been proved right. I am her daughter, no doubt about that.

Do you like your mother? Do you feel warmth towards her? These are quite alien concepts to me. For a long while I refused to believe that this woman who lived in our house was any blood relative of mine. I couldn't see any physical resemblance for a start. Of course, that's all changing now I'm in my fifties, but back when I was a gawky school girl, she didn't look like me at all.

But where does my story start? We have to go back to her childhood, her family, her roots and her aspirations. And as she died without bothering to share them with me, it has been like a detective story, but about my own flesh and blood. I can't tell you why she decided to conceive me or, two years later, my sister, when she clearly found her children a thorough inconvenience.

So *Baggage* is the story of my mother, and through the telling of it I have come to understand a lot more about the woman I had such an uneasy relationship with until the day she died. If only we had been able to talk to each other, things might have been very different. But just as I was moulded by my parents, my own mother took a long and difficult journey from a small Welsh village to a house in suburbia. Now I can see why she was so jealous of all my opportunities. Friendship wasn't ever going to be on the agenda.

Introduction
The Meeting

SHE WAS STRIKING, no doubt about that. The tallest girl at the tea dance at the Winter Gardens in Llandudno, slender, with shoulder-length, dark, wavy hair and a confident manner, a ready smile, chatting with a girlfriend on the edge of the dance floor. He'd been watching her for the last couple of weeks. Now was the time to act. He summoned up his confidence, walked over, and asked her to dance. She sized him up. He was exactly the same height as she was, just as tall and thin. He looked good in his uniform, more interesting than the local lads, that was for sure. Without much hesitation she stubbed out her cigarette, straightened her skirt, looked him up and down, and said, 'All right then.'

Over the next few waltzes she found out that he was called Stan, was in the Royal Signals Corps and had been stationed at nearby Prestatyn and then Rhos on Sea, on the outskirts of Llandudno. They were almost the same age: twenty-four — what a coincidence. She revealed her name was Cherrie, she was a civil servant, working here

in Llandudno for the Board of Trade. Yes, it was a good job, and she was enjoying it because it meant she could visit her relatives living nearby in Llanfairfechan, a small village along the coast, near Bangor. Cherrie was Welsh, even though she had been born in Birkenhead, just outside Liverpool. Her family had all grown up in

Llanfairfechan and Welsh was the first language she had spoken. Stan told her he had been born in Fulham in west London, and had been an electrician before war broke out; his father worked on the new Piccadilly Line and now his parents lived in Southgate in north London. At the end of the evening, Cherrie and Stan arranged to meet again. It was the summer of 1942.

What neither bothered to tell the other was that they were already married, and both their spouses were not far away. Cherrie had only been married less than six months, and Stan a couple of years. But that dance in Llandudno marked the start of a tempestuous relationship in which what wasn't said was more important than what was. When war had been declared on the 3rd of September 1939, the momentous news had thrown people together who feared that they might never see each other again. Men were called up to the armed services and moved around the country, on exercises, in training, in an increasing state of readiness. They could be sent to fight abroad without any warning. Promises were made, marriages took place, engagements announced, all with no real thought beyond the events of that week or month. You could be dead or in another continent by Christmas. The war had brought nothing but good fortune for Cherrie – a better job, new friends, a wider social circle. She'd come a long way from the small stone cottage in Llanfairfechan and sharing a bed with two sisters. Now she wore smart suits, pearls and earrings, considered herself a catch, and had a string of boyfriends who bought her drinks, cigarettes and stockings.

What drove Cherrie Jones was the single idea of self-improvement. She would never forget the day when she was fourteen and her mother had told her she would have to leave school and go out to work. She had cried and cried. How unfair! By common consent she was one of the cleverest girls at the village school in Llanfairfechan. This collection of small stone cottages and Victorian villas faced the island of Anglesey and the Menai Straits to the north, and followed a stream up into the mountains of northern Snowdonia behind, with old farms and hamlets dotted over the surrounding hills. Dominating the skyline was the huge granite quarry, with steep scree slopes dropping to the rocky shoreline. It was a village that had seen ups and downs in its fortunes. In Victorian times rich businessmen had bought land and built grand houses and a church for the English visitors. By the middle of the nineteenth century Llanfairfechan had been transformed from an insular farming community into a tourist resort, with a promenade, shops, guest houses and hotels, grand

detached villas, a recreation ground on the seafront and, most important of all, a station on the main line to Holyhead. But gradually it all changed. The biggest house of all became a secure mental institution, the visitors gradually dwindled, and soon the only employment was the quarry or hill farming.

At the start of the First World War, Cherrie's parents, Thomas and Catherine Mary, had travelled to Manchester and Liverpool in search of work. Catherine was 'in service', working as a maid to a family in Bramhall, on the outskirts of Manchester, while Thomas, whose father had been a gamekeeper in Llangollen, was working at the Cammell Laird shipbuilding yard in Birkenhead, as part of the war effort. They married in Chester in June 1916, and Cherrie was born a year later.

Catherine's family were descended from an amateur historian, Owen Hughes, known as 'the antiquarian', and she had grown up in a white stone cottage high on the hillside of Carreg Fawr, the mountain above Llanfairfechan. One of her brothers, Glyn, was a carpenter, and her other brother, Ifan, worked on the railway. Owen Hughes, who died in 1912, had been interviewed by historians and scholars about the history of their part of Snowdonia — although from humble stock, he had spent his life studying and recording local legends and myths, stories of ghosts, elves and magical spirits. It was even said that the original settlers were a race of fairies who had been driven out by the Welsh centuries ago. But by 1914, the family were

broke and Catherine had been sent away to work in wealthy Manchester as a servant. Her husband Thomas was a striking man — tall, slim and serious. An identical twin, both he and his brother had exactly the same demeanour, prominent ears and premature baldness. It was impossible to tell them apart. Physically, they were slight, not particularly strong, and, like many twins, their personalities were intertwined. In an inward-looking, close-knit community, they had a special bond.

At the end of the war, in 1918, Tom and Catherine moved back to Llanfairfechan with their new baby, settling into Hengai, a grey stone house above the village on the slopes of the mountain. Opposite them, a mile away, lay the quarry, where Tom got a job as a set maker, spending long shifts in all weathers cutting granite blocks. Catherine had more children: a girl, Nancy, then another, Poprin, and two boys, Alan and Eric. In 1923, Cherrie received her first Bible, with a gold clasp and a little envelope with a lock of her baby hair in it. The family would spend every Sunday in the chapel, wearing their best clothes, their hair washed and neatly combed, singing hymns in Welsh before slowly walking the hundred steps up the hill back home.

A series of misfortunes dogged the Jones family. One of the boys, Alan, had always been sickly, with a limp and curvature of the spine. He died aged five, of diphtheria, in an epidemic in which twenty-six other children at the village school also lost their lives. Eric, the other boy, suffered from convulsions, and also died before he went to school. Then another tragedy: the wife of Tom's twin brother Harry died, and their four-year-old daughter Phyllis came to stay with Catherine and Tom so that Harry could work without the worry of raising his child. So Catherine really had her hands full, and Tom's health started to fail. She had four girls at school when he suffered a series of strokes and complained he could hardly breathe. There were days when he got up and begged her not to make him walk all the way down to the river and then up the mountain opposite to work his shift in the quarry. 'Tom, you've got to do it, otherwise we will not eat' was always her reply, and he would slowly drag himself out of bed, wheezing and coughing, and make his way down the lane, summoning up all his strength to do so. Catherine was far, far more robust than he was, cooking, cleaning, balancing the meagre finances and sewing every night by candlelight to make sure everyone looked neat and tidy in chapel. She embroidered pillowcases, tablecloths and blouses. She crocheted blankets and jackets from scraps of wool, and spent hours in the backyard doing the washing with the tub heated by a fire under it, pushing the damp clothes through a mangle, turning a heavy iron handle.

When she was forty-two, Catherine discovered she was pregnant again. By now, Tom was extremely sick. Cherrie had been doing well at school, excelling in the long jump and at running – not surprising as she was the tallest girl at Llanfairfechan National Mixed School. She was quick-witted and intelligent and had won a book by Sir Walter Scott as a prize for her essay on the League of Nations. Everyone had high expectations of her. Now she would have to abandon her education and aspirations and leave school at fourteen and do exactly as Catherine herself had done, travelling to a wealthy suburb of Manchester to work for a middle-class English family. In 1932, Hale, twelve miles from the centre of the city, was being developed as a suburb for the upper middle classes. Professional people and local industrialists were building detached houses with large gardens, on the edge of farmland, where their children would be able to ride and enjoy the clean air, and attend one of the private schools in the immediate vicinity. The first house in Carlton Road in Hale was built in 1929, and all those that followed

Elliot, and Violet was enrolled at the local school. The Jones family was in exile in the suburbs of Manchester.

Cherrie and her two sisters were enjoying themselves, cycling to local beauty spots and going skating in Manchester. She had grown from a shy teenager, accustomed to insular village life surrounded by relatives and clannish neighbours, into an attractive young woman of eighteen, blossoming in middle-class surroundings, in a pleasant part of the countryside with plenty of amenities, from tennis courts to river walks. Cherrie read a lot and was very conscious of her lack of formal education. In the back cover of one of her old school books, the Walter Scott novel she'd won as a prize, she carefully copied out a romantic poem by Robert Louis Stevenson, entitled 'To Minnie', and dated it, 1st July 1936:

> The Red Room with the giant bed
> Where none but elders lay their head
> The little room where you and I
> Did for a while together lie
> And, simple suitor, I your hand
> In decent marriage did demand.

Clearly, Cherrie wanted a better life than her parents had had, and one of the best ways to improve her lot would be to marry well. Daydreaming of meeting Mr Right while looking after her young charges, this poem must have struck a chord. Stuck in a poky little servant's room in Hale with little or no privacy, she yearned for a decent job, with more money to buy nice clothes and makeup. She wanted the glamorous kind of life she'd seen at the cinema and read about in romantic novels. She wanted passion, sex. Cherrie was a real livewire, who loved to dance and have fun whenever she got a night off. With her striking looks, she wasn't short of admirers and on one of her local outings either to the cinema or skating a couple of years later she met George Ardern, whose father was a butcher in Marple Bridge, just outside Stockport about ten miles away. George was two years younger than Cherrie, and a joiner, but what particularly impressed her was that he had his own sports car, an MG, and could whisk her back to Llanfairfechan to show off to the relatives.

With the outbreak of war in 1939, George joined the army and, on the spur of the moment, in 1941, they decided to get married. The ceremony took place in November 1941 and Cherrie gave her address as 30 Carlton Road, Hale. It was an awkward arrangement because the only time the newlyweds could ever spend together was when George got forty-eight hours' leave and they would go back to Wales, where her mother was now working for a family in a grand house on the sea front. Catherine had been forced to take this job because it included accommodation for her and Violet, and they were homeless because another relative was living in their house higher up in the village. Cherrie obviously married George Ardern so that they could consummate their relationship – but where? Perhaps in boarding houses and at relatives' cottages in Wales, at best a snatched night on one of their days off. Perhaps at his brother's farm outside Chester, where Violet spent some weeks on holiday. For the whole of their married life they never lived together, and soon meeting was even more difficult as George was being sent around the country by the army.

As the war intensified Cherrie decided to leave the Manchester area and her job in Hale and return to Llanfairfechan before she was called up. She tried working

in an ammunition factory in Colwyn Bay, but hated
wearing her hair in a headscarf. She thought the work

of army camp. Cherrie was excellent company, sharp and funny, but Stan may not have realised that he was just one of many admirers she had on the back burner, including a Dutch sailor stationed on the Orme. Cherrie would take her six-year-old sister Violet along as a sort of chaperone on these wartime dates, and seemed to like to maintain an air of mystery about her exact status. On the day she met Stan, she didn't bother to tell him about her other men friends or the fact she was already married, although, like many marriages of the time, the two people involved may have had very different motives. Apart from both wanting to enjoy sex without disapproval, Cherrie wanted to escape from Hale, and perhaps George thought that this attractive woman would make a fine wife and eventually a mother. But Cherrie, under Eileen's tuition, was already changing into a very different girl from the sweet young nanny who had captured the eye of George Ardern. She clearly enjoyed the money and freedom that her new job brought her, and through Eileen she was making new friends, going to concerts and widening her horizons.

When Cherrie and Eileen were transferred to work in Manchester, at the Board of Trade offices in Deansgate,

Cherrie cut her ties with Llanfairfechan and the Welsh relatives and the two girls shared a flat together in Moss Side. Cherrie certainly didn't bother to tell George, or his parents, who were only ten miles away, that she was dating other men and being unfaithful to her husband. But Stan, too, had omitted to tell Cherrie everything about himself that day they first met dancing in Llandudno. Who knows why, perhaps he found her so attractive he may have worried he might lose her. Stan had a wife in Liverpool. A couple of months after war had been declared, on the 4th of November 1939, he had married Nancy Siddall, an aircraft inspector, in Gloucester, where he was working as an electrician. Nancy was twenty-three, two years older than he was, and they had just set up home together when he was called up in March 1940. After he joined the Royal Signals Corps they must have spent very little time together. Stan moved from Prestatyn to Chester to Llandudno, spending some time in Penrith in Cumbria. He does not seem to have ever returned to see his wife, spending most of his leave with Cherrie in North Wales or Manchester.

In 1944 Cherrie's mother Catherine eventually got the family cottage in Llanfairfechan back and took a job in St Winifred's School in the village as a cook and cleaner because it gave her free food and the meagre wages supplemented her widow's pension of ten shillings a week. The rent for the cottage took six shillings and so every little helped. Cherrie sent her money whenever she could, as the family had no breadwinner. By now Stan had been sent abroad, sailing to India and then on to Burma. Cherrie took Violet to Eileen's relatives in Bournemouth on holiday. Meanwhile, she carried on going for a drink with anyone who took her fancy. Secretly, though, she was besotted by Stan, who was writing to her from the Far East.

Stan was always to be an enigma to Cherrie, who had grown up in a very small cottage crammed with children, in poverty. He was an only child, born directly after the First World War, to two people, Clara and William, who seemed to have very little in common. Clara was stiff, formal, quiet and deeply suspicious of anyone she didn't know. She seemed cold and was not tactile in the slightest, never showing any sign of physical affection for either

her husband or her son in public. She doted on her son, however, and utterly spoilt him. Stan inherited her lack of physicality, her sense of order, her bossiness. William Bull was an ebullient easy-going character, who took a job as a train driver and was a popular man at work and in his street. Deprived of a decent education, he built a small laboratory at home and spent hours building gadgets and conducting experiments. Stan spent his first years in his grandparents' house in Rectory Road in Fulham, but before he started at Holman Hunt Primary School in the New King's Road, the family moved into their own terraced house in nearby Foskett Road. There were plenty of Bull family members who lived in Fulham, and one of Stan's distant relatives, Harry, had captained a West London Schoolboys team in 1910 – the highlight of his sporting career was playing for the England Schoolboys team against Scotland in 1911. Like his famous relative, Stan loved sport, particularly speedway racing and football. He took up cycling and joined a club, spending weekends cycling to Brighton and back in a day. When he left school he started work as an electrician's mate, soon learning his craft. He got a job with a firm of contractors which took him travelling all over the country, and was working on a job in Gloucester when he met Nancy. Meanwhile, his parents had left Fulham and bought a brand-new house which they named 'Electra' in Southgate near the end of the Piccadilly Line. It had a long garden which William soon turned into a series of vegetable plots, planting fruit trees and making a pond on which he kept ducks. There was a chicken coop and a greenhouse for tomatoes and marrows. The Bulls were to be more or less completely self-sufficient throughout the Second World War.

At the end of 1945, Stan returned to England from Burma and was eventually discharged from the army in March 1946. He had achieved the rank of sergeant and received a glowing commendation from his lieutenant colonel: 'An electrician in Civil Life who has adapted himself to Line Communication equipment and reached a particularly high standard in both exchange installation and underground cable construction . . . has excellent organising ability and a clear mind for planning.' Plan number one was most definitely not to return home to Electra and the watchful eye of his suffocating mother in

Southgate, or to his wife Nancy for that matter.

Cherrie and Eileen were now working for the Civil Service in London and had rented a flat together above a parade of shops near Hanger Lane tube station in Ealing, west London. Stan turned up, and moved in with them. Within a month Cherrie was pregnant. Stan's mother would have been appalled, and he immediately went up to Liverpool and persuaded Nancy to give him a divorce, which was granted in November, a month before I was born at Chiswick Maternity Hospital on 27 December at 12.30 a.m. Our first outing after I was brought home was to Nana Bull's in Southgate for tea one Sunday, where I was much admired.

Whether Cherrie had told Stan about her husband George by then, no one knows. Certainly George didn't know about the new baby, and Cherrie didn't go and see him or his parents while she was pregnant. It would have been easy to find them, but for some reason (possibly fear that she would not get the divorce she wanted) she did not go. And so I was born with my mother already in Nana Bull's bad books, as her beloved Stan was living in sin with a married woman, a situation which was to get worse over the next six years. Nana, unhappy about Stan's divorce, seemed to blame Cherrie, whereas it was Stan who had got her pregnant. Cherrie, with a tiny baby, discovered that my father, always very organised and slightly bossy, had to be the centre of attention – that was how he'd grown up. Everything around him had to be just perfect for him. Cherrie's troubles were just beginning.

Soon after I was born in 1946, my parents bought a terraced house in Fulham, which had belonged to relatives of my father. They had no money at all, and had to pay £800 to purchase it, a considerable sum for an electrician. Built in 1891, it was on three floors, with fine red, cream and black tiles forming geometric patterns in the hall, stained-glass windows in the front door, bay windows to the front, and a small garden at the rear. Fulham was full of Victorian streets like ours, all built between 1860 and 1900, with larger, more palatial versions of the same houses on main roads, in the Peterborough Estate towards the river, and around Parsons Green. The mortgage of £4 a month was hard to pay on the small wages my father earned as an electrician employed by a company in Victoria, and my mother could hardly work with a newborn baby. And so Eileen (who I was to grow up calling Auntie Eileen), Mum's best friend through the war years and her former flatmate in Ealing, came to stay and paid rent, sharing one of the two bedrooms in our bit of the house with me. The top two floors, including the bathroom and the indoor toilet, were rented out to a bus conductor, Cyril Redman, and his family, which included two children. We had to use the outside toilet in the garden, wash in the sink in the scullery, and were able to use the bathroom with its frightening gas water heater for a couple of hours on Sunday afternoons.

My mother was still very much in my father's thrall – perhaps the fact he had been out of the country had intensified their relationship and they had not spent too much time together during their courtship, like many wartime romances. Even though to outsiders he could seem extremely domineering and bossy, she still found him glamorous and confident, and was content to let him make all the rules, from what time they would eat, to insisting she that she wore an apron in the kitchen to serve meals.

She was probably looking forward to returning to work part-time when, less than eighteen months after I was born, she discovered she was pregnant again. During this pregnancy she felt particularly depressed and was outraged to come into the kitchen in early December 1948 and discover Eileen enjoying an intimate moment with my father. They may or may not have been embracing – perhaps they were just drinking or smoking together after work – but, whatever my mother saw, she was absolutely convinced they were having an affair. Eileen was still in the Civil Service, working in Victoria Street, near the headquarters of my dad's company, so perhaps they had come home from work together. Eight months pregnant and completely distraught, my mother wrote to her mother in North Wales and begged her to send Violet to London to keep her company. She could not continue to live with my father without her sister by her side.

Violet was fifteen and a half, and was the only member of the family to have passed the Eleven-plus – she'd gained a place at Bangor Grammar School and was soon to sit her matriculation. Her dreams and aspirations were all swept aside in a bid to avert a family scandal, as Nain, my Welsh granny, withdrew Violet from school and put her on the train to London on December 19th. Two weeks later, on January 2nd, 1949, my sister Pat was born. When she was brought home from the maternity hospital on Parsons Green, I shared a bedroom with Violet while my new sister slept in a cot next to my parents' bed.

Eileen moved out and rented a room in Notting Hill Gate. She was given the deep chill treatment for several years but, as she was my godmother, and my mother found her entertaining company, the past was eventually set aside and Eileen rejoined the family circle.

Years later my mother was to cruelly tell my sister that she wished she'd never given birth to her, and that by then her relationship with my father was on the wane. This was not necessarily true, but discovering him with Eileen had definitely changed things. She told Pat years later that she couldn't get an abortion, but whether she actually tried was another matter.

I

Married in Secret

THERE WAS EXCITED talk in our kitchen one morning, as my mother and her sister furiously chattered away in Welsh as usual, with the local newspaper unfolded on the oilcloth of the table in front of them – but I could make out some words in English. 'Jabber jabber jabber launderette jabber Bendix jabber' was how this big news event sounded to me, aged four or so. That afternoon, I was strapped into a pushchair and wheeled along the Fulham Road past the cheery greengrocer's where we used to buy our vegetables every week, past the off licence, the newsagent's, and into the Broadway itself. We stopped in front of a plate-glass window. I was confused: this wasn't a shop – nothing was on sale. Inside I stared at large, white, rectangular, shiny metal boxes; the front of each was pierced by a porthole with a chrome trim. These boxes were pulsating with life, chugging and gurgling away, rocking gently and whirring. In their stomachs, behind the circular glass windows, I could see tangled masses of wet material rotating forwards and back.

Inside the door, my mother unhooked a large bag from behind me and handed some money to a woman in an overall at the counter. Mum put some change in her purse and was given a plastic container of powder and a couple of metal tokens. Entranced, I was lifted out of my push-chair and placed in a moulded plastic seat, facing a silent machine whose door was open. What on earth was going to happen? Dragged from the bag, loads of sheets were unfolded and pushed through the hatch, which was slammed shut. Then she poured the powder into a drawer on the top of the machine, slid it shut, stuck a couple of tokens in a slot and pressed a button.

Immediately the machine roared violently into life. I was open-mouthed. It was like being at a birthday party – I expected music to start playing like it did on the radio in our kitchen, or at the very least puppets or a conjuror to appear through the porthole, but nothing except endless whooshing and whirring happened for the next hour and a quarter while I stared hypnotically at the white foam in the porthole and dozed off from time to time and Mum read a magazine. Then, when the machine had noisily clanked to a halt, the wet stuff inside it was taken out and loaded into the top of another white box, more tokens were slid in, and a lot of high-pitched spinning noises erupted for ten minutes or so before it, too, shuddered to a standstill. Finally the dry sheets were taken out, shaken and folded, and placed back in their original bag which was hooked on the back of my pushchair. I had my hat, coat and gloves put back on, was firmly strapped in and we slowly made our way back along the Fulham Road, which was now bathed in pools of light as the evening set in, home for tea and crumpets. My first visit to a launderette was over.

Having read in the *Fulham Chronicle* that Bendix were opening a branch in Fulham Broadway, Mum had decided to forgo the cheap bagwash (only a shilling a week, and our clothes went in a sack with those of our upstairs tenants, the Redmans) at the Sunlight Laundry around the corner and pay the borough's first launderette a visit. There was always the risk of incurring my father's wrath over unnecessary expenditure, but she would be able to boast that she was the first person in Elmstone Road to participate in this new and fashionable labour-saving experience. After a few trips the excitement would diminish but, as we didn't have a television, I found the hour or so spent watching our sheets and towels being washed in a machine every week totally mesmeric.

In the early 1950s I seemed to live in a very small world in Fulham. My first memories of being wheeled anywhere in my pushchair were to council offices about a mile away on the Fulham Palace Road where my mother would get her ration books stamped. As money was extremely short in our household, she combined bringing up two small children with a whole variety of part-time jobs over the next decade to boost the family finances, from working in Marks and Spencer in the North End Road to dishing out school dinners at the Roman Catholic Servite School at the Chelsea end of the Fulham Road. Her first full-time job, when we had started at secondary school, was in an office in the Magneta vacuum cleaner factory on Parsons Green Lane.

In spite of limited resources, my parents were determined that I should learn ballet and tap, in the hope that perhaps I might develop some grace and style, and perhaps follow in the footsteps of my godmother, Auntie Eileen, who claimed to have been a ballet dancer at Covent Garden when she was younger. So my mother would take me back twice a week to the Fulham Palace Road, near where we'd gone for the ration books, to dance classes in a prefab. It didn't take long to discover that I had absolutely no sense of balance and was going to be far too tall to be a ballet dancer. Soon afterwards, the tap teacher kindly told my mother I had no sense of rhythm and was a

washout at that as well. My sister persevered, but eventually abandoned her classes too.

But if I failed at ballet, I was a whizz at cards. Both parents loved board games like ludo, snakes and ladders, draughts and Chinese checkers, and were particularly competitive at card games. From a very early age my sister and I would be roped in, spending hour after hour around the wooden kitchen table in the evenings, with the wireless on. My father was a huge fan of radio comedy (funny, as he didn't really have any sense of humour as far as we could make out) – Jimmy Edwards and The Glums in *Take It from Here*, *Hancock's Half Hour*, and Peter Brough and Archie Andrews. I could never understand the appeal of a ventriloquist on the radio, but Peter Brough was a huge hit then, and my parents found the inane ramblings of his little doll Archie, who wore a school cap and a striped blazer, absolutely side-splitting. Mostly the four of us played gin rummy, and we children were not allowed any leeway or relaxing of the rules because we were at least thirty years younger than the two adults. It was all rather nerve-racking as I had to focus on playing my hand well at the same time as following the plot on the radio, but worth the effort because it meant that we could stretch our bedtimes by half an hour if we spun out playing our hands.

Fulham in the 1950s was a cosmopolitan but tight-knit place, just a series of villages grouped around various estates and parades of shops, with all the Catholic children attending their own schools, from primary to senior colleges. We hardly knew any Catholics at all – they seemed an exotic race to us Church of England worshippers at St Dionis Church in Parsons Green, like French or Italians. Coming from a similarly small community in North Wales, my mother must have felt lonely and isolated, unlike my father who had grown up less than a quarter of a mile away from where we now lived. She particularly missed being able to speak Welsh, and would travel all over the borough looking for other Welsh people to chat to. Luckily there were several dairies run by people called Jones (her maiden name) – although they were not related – and one was just near us in the Fulham Road. She would spend hours in there talking this mysterious lingo while she bought a pint of milk or some eggs.

My mother's closest friend in the years before I went to school was her sister Violet. The other two sisters, Nancy and Poprin, were married, living in Birmingham and Manchester. Before she moved in with us permanently, Violet and Nain used to come and visit regularly. There was one memorable Christmas when a large chunk of the marble fireplace in the front room fell off during the festivities and my granny bled profusely from a nasty cut on her leg. A furious row between my parents ensued as my embarrassed mother blamed my father for something which was quite clearly not his fault. Soon my father had ruthlessly demolished this splendid piece of Victoriana and replaced it with a home-made, dreary, brick fireplace, which had no pointy corners or bits which might cause family ructions.

Whatever had happened, our family now divided into two camps, the English and the Welsh speakers. We got a budgerigar, and my mother taught it Welsh. I was so ashamed, I never invited anyone round from school. I thought they might think we were all mad at 18 Elmstone Road. As far as I knew, there were no other Welsh speakers at Peterborough Primary School and, being anxious to fit in, I didn't want to appear too 'different' to anyone else. My mother now had her sister as her main ally in our house and at mealtimes the English and the Welsh speakers sat at separate ends of the table. My mother's Welshness was reinforced by the presence of her sister, and they happily jabbered away for hours on end in their mother tongue. As I grew older and my Welsh grandmother suffered increasingly from bronchitis, she too would come to London for months on end and there were three Welsh speakers and a budgie holding forth.

My father was a distant character who clearly wished he'd produced a couple of boys, not girls. In their different ways both of our parents seemed like strangers rather than our nearest relatives. My sister and I soon took to staring at them like animals at the pet shop. We were not particularly feminine little things either, both being raucous tomboys who loved games and competitions. But that was not enough to please our father – we weren't real boys. One Christmas when we were six and four was a disaster, because we were given a doll each. I wanted Meccano, or a Hornby Dublo train, and within a week had ripped the arms off my dolly in a temper. My mother took the wretched thing to the Dolls' Hospital off Fulham Broadway to be repaired, but I only pulled her limbs off again in a matter of days. That was my first and last doll, and the next Christmas I had my wish, a Meccano set, and used it to build a scale model of the Blackpool Tower, aided by my dad, who obviously thoroughly enjoyed such pursuits.

In another attempt to treat me like the son he wished he'd had, as soon as I was eight he would take me every

other Saturday to see the Fulham football team. We'd take the bus to Craven Cottage by the Thames at the western end of Bishop's Park, and I'd scream and shout for Johnny Haynes, our star player. These were exciting times for Fulham as they'd made it up to the First Division. I would stand on the terraces in the coldest of weather, wrapped up in a club scarf and thick woolly gloves. In those days the terraces were perfectly safe, full of fathers with their children, drinking Bovril and eating hot dogs at half time.

On Wednesday evenings during the season we'd take the tube train from Parsons Green to Wimbledon to speedway racing, where the local star was Barry Briggs. Again I would be playing the part of the son he wished he'd had. My sister and my mother rarely accompanied us on these outings to Craven Cottage or Speedway – it just wasn't their scene. An exception was the memorable Saturday night in July when the whole family travelled to Wembley Stadium to see my dad's hero Barry Briggs win the world title.

Speedway had a smell and an atmosphere that was so special: the misty winter evenings, the smell of the cinders and the fuel, the roar of the tyres and the squealing of the brakes. The programmes in which my dad and I would carefully fill in every lap time, the enamelled club badges I would religiously collect, the striped bobble hats in our team's colours, and the club scarves. Before the war, my father had worked as a mechanic when speedway was held at what became the Chelsea football stadium. Speedway and football were the only times I ever really felt he was enjoying himself but even then he was not someone given to lavish or spontaneous expressions of extrovert behaviour. I was simply treated as his companion, and as I grew older I was replaced by his friends from the office. In the end he would purchase a season ticket to Fulham and go alone. The other source of pleasure for him was gardening or, more specifically, growing vegetables. Like his father he liked nothing better that spending a Sunday afternoon smoking continuously while digging his allotment in Bishop's Park. He would spend hours there, tending an immaculate plot of potatoes, leeks, onions and carrots, and we were most definitely not welcome. But these home-grown vegetables helped the family budget go further, even if it meant he was not available to us for long periods of time.

To save money, Mum would walk a considerable distance with a pram to get a bag of cheap coke from the gasworks off Wandsworth Bridge Road, and each Christmas Dad would leave buying a turkey in the North End Road market until the very last minute in the hope of scoring a bargain. But one Christmas Eve, when I was about six, he failed in his mission and returned home at 6 p.m. with a goose with all its feathers on. My mother went ballistic, and started screaming and shouting at the top of her voice. My sister and I were ordered to our bedroom, as she seized the bird by the neck and started hitting Dad around the head with it. We could hear the row through the floorboards, and a lot of pans were banged about and chopping boards thrown. Finally Mum stormed off to bed and Dad had to pluck the goose himself in the scullery. On Christmas morning we awoke to find our stockings filled, but she refused to get out of bed until midday in protest, and Dad had to cook the lunch himself. It was, as usual, consumed in silence.

Auntie Vi had found a job at the Gas, Light and Coke Company in Victoria earning £2 a week. She was allowed time off to complete her school work, and paid my parents half her pitiful pay towards her keep. Her biggest fun was dancing on Saturday nights with her workmate Joan, at Caxton Hall in Victoria or at Fulham Town Hall. Violet was extremely pretty and vivacious, and my mother became like her stepmother, insisting she be home by 10 p.m. Vi would save up for the £3 return train fare back up to Wales to see Nain regularly, to escape from the rules and regulations of 18 Elmstone Road. After a year of dancing with different men in London and seeing the local lads on her trips to Wales, she became engaged to Ray,

who had just finished training to be a policeman and was stationed locally in Walham Grove. A year later, they were married at the church in Fulham Broadway, and I was a bridesmaid. No wonder my mother looked wistful in the photographs – she and my father were still hiding a huge secret from all their friends: my mother's first husband George Ardern had still not given her a divorce, and she and my father had been unable to get married.

Life continued in Elmstone Road much as before. My Auntie Vi and Uncle Ray moved into a flat in number 20, right next door to us, and so my mother saw her every single day – they were closer than ever. Vi continued to work for the gas company and my sister and I would spend hours next door with them both. She and Ray seemed so much more fun than our own mum and dad (she was not even twenty and Ray not much older). Meal times now at number 18 became a nightmare. My father would bellow, 'GET YOUR ELBOWS OFF THE TABLE' at everyone, including my mother, whose apron had to be spotless at all times. We were made to sit at the table in the kitchen for hours until all the food on our plates was eaten. I took to stuffing things I loathed, like butter beans, in my socks or pockets when he wasn't looking. My sister had a series of sinus problems and was inclined to make a snuffling noise (which she couldn't hear) while she ate. 'IF YOU MAKE THAT RUDDY SOUND ONE MORE TIME YOU'LL BE FINISHING YOUR MEAL STANDING UP IN THE SCULLERY,' Dad would shout, and two meals out of four my sister would be ordered from the room. Mum was cowed by his rages but, when angry, she could certainly give as good as she got. Consequently, when her sister was next door and out of earshot, life at 18 Elmstone Road was often punctuated by frosty silences interspersed with short screaming matches. Neither parent would ever admit they were wrong, or apologise to the other. They were both extremely stubborn.

Throughout the 1950s most households in central London had coal fires, and the smog was tremendous. My mother and I walked all the way home from the Fulham Road in Chelsea one day, unable to see more than six feet in front of us. The air was thick and foul-smelling, full of trapped gases. The feeling of living in a horror film increased one smoggy afternoon when a huge thunderstorm erupted.

As the lightning forked overhead, my mother could stand it no longer and fled to the cellar, where my father kept all his tools and had a workbench on which he mended our shoes. When he returned from work drenched at 6 o'clock and found my sister and me cowering in the kitchen alone, he was even more frightening than the storm. 'WHERE'S YOUR MOTHER?' he yelled, his face turning an unattractive shade of red. 'In the cellar,' we whispered. He flung the door to the basement open as the rain teemed down outside the kitchen windows in the backyard, screaming, 'WHAT THE HELL IS GOING ON? WHAT KIND OF EXAMPLE DO YOU THINK YOU'RE SETTING? GET UP HERE RIGHT AWAY.' My mother emerged snivelling and shaking and my sister and I both promptly started weeping too. 'FOR GOD'S SAKE PULL YOURSELF TOGETHER, WOMAN,' he ranted, to no avail. We never did discover what had made my mother so frightened of lightning, and years later when we moved to Ealing I once found her trying to cram herself into the hall cupboard under the stairs during a storm. Luckily Dad was out – 'Don't tell your father,' she pleaded with me. No chance of that; I hadn't spoken to him on any personal matter for years by then (chats at football and speedway were limited to the factual) and I wasn't going to start now.

A couple of years after my Auntie Vi's wedding, my mother disappeared for a couple of days. My sister and I weren't told where she'd gone. She had travelled by train up to Manchester on a desperate mission to persuade her husband to divorce her, staying with her sister Poprin in Sale. She was successful and the papers finally came through in early July 1954, citing her adultery with Stanley Bull, my father. Barely two months later, on the 18th of September, in a registry office in Barnet near my grandparents' home, my mum and dad finally tied the knot, with my Uncle Ray and granddad as witnesses. By then they were thirty-six and thirty-seven years old – less than a year between their birthdays. My sister and I, aged five and seven, weren't there, and were not informed. There were no photographs taken, no celebrations and nothing to record this momentous occasion, apart from a wedding certificate, which my mother kept locked away until her death. My sister and I were never informed that both my parents had previous marriages which had ended in divorce until after my father's death. Even then we were shown shortened copy versions of our birth certificates, which Mum had got in 1951, which only stated our names and dates of birth. On our medical records and all other childhood documentation my mother went to enormous lengths to hide the fact that both my sister and I were illegitimate. The reason was simple: she felt that she had let my father and his family down in some way. It was perfectly obvious that unlike all our neighbours there were no wedding photographs on display in the front room of our house, and she must have worried about what people would think.

My father never failed to make everyone else feel inferior and my mother was increasingly cowed into submission by this mini dictator. In many ways she adopted his worst traits herself, discarding people when they were no longer of any use, and living in a very self-contained world where they spent most of their time together or she could only do things he approved of. She would go shopping each Saturday with Violet for a few brief hours of freedom, but would remove any unauthorised purchases like clothing from their carrier bags and stuff them into her handbag to avoid rows before he arrived. She would not be allowed to visit friends unless she could be sure of getting home in time to cook his supper every night, even though she had a job and work friends of her own. She learnt to drive, but he so derided her motoring skills that once she had passed the test she never drove again.

These rows became more frequent as the years went on, and on several occasions she stormed out of the house, taking my sister with her, staying with one of my father's aunts in Earls Court. The early division of our family unit into the Welsh and non-Welsh speakers had subtly changed into one where my mother used my sister as a pawn in her disputes with my father. They would be gone for several days, and then she would return without warning, resuming all the set routines as before. They were locked into a relationship it was too late for her to get out of. In family photographs he would stand stiffly apart from the rest of the family group, rigid and formal. Physical contact was kept to a minimum – I couldn't remember him ever cuddling or hugging me, it wasn't his style. Gradually my mother turned from being lively and extrovert into a quieter, more passive being when he was around. She could still laugh and joke, smoking and drinking with work friends and her sisters, but in front of him she became the subservient partner. My sister and I soon realised too that life went a lot more easily if you didn't argue back to him, and didn't do anything to upstage him. We gradually retreated into our own separate worlds inside 18 Elmstone Road – things were just simpler that way. I didn't talk much to my sister, as in my mind my mother had subtly set her against me in the battle for supremacy with my dad.

2

School Days

I SAT IN THE silent classroom alone after all the other children had gone home, concentrating intently on a white piece of card propped up on the desk next to my exercise book. It made no sense whatsoever, covered with line after line of loops, forming an elegant pattern, but containing no words. Totally focused on my blue-stained left forefinger and thumb, which shook slightly as they gripped a slim brown wooden stem, I dipped the metal nib at the end of it into a little china pot of ink on the desk and slowly, grimly, tried to copy the mysterious loops from the card. Before a minute was up, the pen had keeled over as if driven by a manic force out of my control and even more ink splodged on to my fingers. A large blot ruined the pristine page of my notebook. An authoritarian voice boomed out from behind me: 'Janet Bull, you must persevere. NO ONE at Peterborough Junior School has ever sat the Eleven-plus in pencil, and you are not going to be the first. Carry on, PLEASE.' I bent over the desk, jammed the pen back between my fingers and started again.

It was just before Christmas 1957. I was to spend hours in detention after classes had ended each day before I mastered the art of using a pen — funny, really, because my school reports up to then always claimed I had excellent writing, but that was when pencil was permitted, in the lower forms.

Peterborough Primary and Junior School, where I was enrolled in the summer of 1951, aged four, rose like a glorious grand palace towering over all the houses on the Earl of Peterborough's Estate at the southern end of Fulham where it reached the Thames. Built in 1901, the year of Queen Victoria's death, no money had been stinted in its construction. With high, pointed gables, turrets, large redbrick chimneys and terracotta ornamentation, it was the biggest building I'd even seen. Girls, Boys and attendants.' From then on I stuffed any food I couldn't eat in my pockets and tipped it out in the playground later.

There were plenty of unruly children in the school, and most of them came from working-class homes like mine — their fathers were milkmen, lorry drivers, painters, plumbers, shoe repairers. Out of a class of forty, perhaps two or three would have middle-class dads who were accountants, civil servants or lawyers. Most people did not own their homes, but lived in rented accommodation. One girl in our class used to urinate on the floor regularly during class, and when her mother was summoned to remove her she strode shouting into the classroom and punched the teacher in the face. The police escorted them off the premises and we never saw them again. The boys in the junior school could get very boisterous — one afternoon there was a pitched battle in Studdridge Street when they took on their counterparts from the Catholic Holy Cross School a few streets away, wielding branches and bits of wood. During the 1950s there was a 'war' between several of the families who ran scrap-metal yards in Fulham, and one of the children in my class had the front of their father's premises strafed with gunfire as a warning. My mother and father told my sister and me not to talk to anyone who lived in a council flat, but they seemed unaware of the fact that some of the kids at school who lived in houses were pretty frightening in their own way. Primary and junior school playgrounds were not places where you wanted to look too different, or stand out in any way, in case you got picked on. At least people in council flats had their own indoor toilets and bathrooms.

At the end of my first year a magical event happened. We were told to be very tidy and smart the next day as the school had a special visitor. On July 17th 1952 a woman in a black suit, wearing a posh hat and gloves, and carrying a large handbag, got out of a huge car and was cheered by crowds of people. She entered the playground and was met by a man wearing a fancy gold chain, and walked along a line-up of all our teachers, who performed a series of bobs in rotation. She then walked over to our gardens (I was far too young to have any idea of what was happening) and chatted to some of the older children, who were definitely on best behaviour.

Queen Mary, the Queen Mother, was paying us a

visit on behalf of the London Flower Lovers' League. From then on I grew nasturtiums in pots every summer and daffodils in pots every winter, collecting countless certificates for my weedy specimens. But she never returned.

The next big excitement was the morning we were all gathered in the large assembly hall and told that soon we would have a new Queen. The best thing was that we would get time off school for parties and the Coronation (whatever that was – I was only six and had no grasp of matters of state). We had a party in Elmstone Road, with a big table down the middle of the street, and my mother took my little sister and me on the Underground to see the Coronation procession from Westminster Abbey. We got to Park Lane in the morning – it was not to pass for at least four hours, and I managed to get a top slot right at the front of the crowd to get a brief glimpse of an incredible gold coach with a woman inside wearing glittering clothes and a crown, accompanied by endless men on white horses. I dreamt about it for weeks afterwards. At school we got given special china beakers and propelling pencils to mark the event.

At school my reports were excellent, filled with 'V.G.'

(very good), with only the occasional bit of carping about my lack of concentration and forgetfulness of my duties as a monitor. When I was about six my eyes were tested after my parents realised I couldn't see the numbers on the front of the 22 bus in Fulham Road. Eureka! I went straight to the top of the class – I could read the blackboard at last. From then on, it didn't really matter that the other kids called me Olive Oyl because I was tall and skinny, or poked fun at my glasses, I was smarter than they were and could tolerate the teasing. I became obsessed with winning at everything, from cards to spelling to maths to rounders. I was a voracious reader and everyone in the family gave me books for my birthday and at Christmas, from pot-boilers like *What Katy Did Next* to *The Coral Island* by R.M. Ballantyne. There was an essay competition run by Brooke Bond tea at school and the subject was 'kindness to animals'. Even at that age I was a complete cynic, and cobbled together a heart-rending tale entitled 'A day in the life of a seaside donkey', winning a certificate and book tokens.

Apart from school, my life revolved around the large redbrick St Dionis Church on Parsons Green. I had been christened there in 1947, when we'd first arrived in Fulham, with Auntie Eileen as my godmother. My mother belonged to the Young Wives' Club and the Mothers' Union – it was where she had made all her friends when she was a new arrival in the neighbourhood. The Rev. Stewart Dumphries ran a busy empire, with Sunday School, Cubs and Scouts, a youth club, a junior club and a choir as well as Eucharist during the week and weddings and baptisms on the weekends. The church hall, a matching Victorian brick building on the opposite side of St Dionis Road, was busy most nights of the week. From the age of seven I was sent to Sunday School every Sunday afternoon

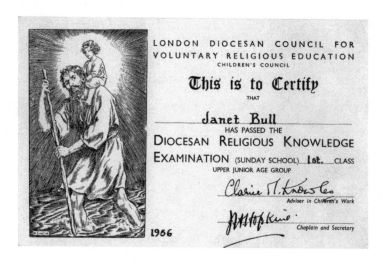

LONDON DIOCESAN COUNCIL FOR VOLUNTARY RELIGIOUS EDUCATION
CHILDREN'S COUNCIL

This is to Certify
THAT

Janet Bull

HAS PASSED THE
DIOCESAN RELIGIOUS KNOWLEDGE EXAMINATION (SUNDAY SCHOOL) 1st. CLASS
UPPER JUNIOR AGE GROUP

Clarice M. Knowles
Adviser in Children's Work

J H Hopkins
Chaplain and Secretary

1966

between 3 and 4 o'clock, with my sister when she was old enough, and was awarded certificates in Religious Knowledge, passing the yearly examinations in the New Testament at the top level. I won a novel as a prize for my regular attendance, an extraordinary story about a boy called Bim who was kidnapped in China and held to ransom.

My parents must have been thrilled to have the house to themselves while we were at church as it gave them time at home alone, possibly for sex. Sunday always followed exactly the same ritual. The morning was taken up with chores, and the radio was on continuously throughout our meal of overcooked vegetables, meat and potatoes, eaten in the kitchen by Dad wearing a shirt and V-neck sweater, Mum a clean dress and apron, and my sister and me in our best dresses, ready for Sunday School. *Two-Way Family Favourites* followed by *The Billy Cotton Band Show*, followed by *Round the Horne* while we washed up. We would put on our best overcoats and shoes, comb our hair and then walk down the road to the church while they settled down with cups of tea and Peter Noble's *MovieGoRound* on the old Home Service – as the music started we were shooed out of the front door. How I longed to be transported to the set of Dirk Bogarde's latest offering, instead of studying the good deeds of Jesus and his ruddy disciples. As I got older I loathed Sunday School, seeing it as an extension of my Monday-to-Friday education into my precious free time. I would rebel by taking the Underground to South Kensington afterwards, walking along the subway tunnel to emerge at the Science Museum where I would scour the galleries looking for boys to sneer at and shout at. The coal mine was a surefire winner, and I was thrown out of the museum on more than one occasion for making too much noise as I aimlessly kicked litter bins and played with the control knobs on models of mining machinery.

I would go to the junior club in St Dionis Church Hall after school between 6.30 and 7.30 on Wednesdays, when we basically just ran around and made plenty of noise, and when I was ten or eleven I qualified for the youth club, which meant a lot of standing around while records were played looking sneery at any boys brave enough to turn up. There was much excitement when two boys who had sung in the choir (one of them had played in a skiffle group at the youth club) formed a duo and called themselves the Allisons. They beat 600 other hopefuls and won a talent competition organised by *Disc* pop newspaper, and eventually came second in the Eurovision Song Contest in 1961, singing 'Are You Sure?'.

From the age of five to twelve my sister and I were St Dionis stalwarts. We had parties in the hall with jelly and cakes at Christmas, and trips to south-coast seaside resorts like Worthing and Bognor in coaches on a Saturday each summer. I was confirmed in June 1959, aged twelve, somewhat reluctantly (my parents insisted on it), and I never attended Communion again. My mother had given me a Bible as an Easter present three years earlier, hoping to instil a sense of moral purpose in my life.

Even though I gradually found church suffocating, the Sunday once a month when we went to family matins at 11 o'clock was a big event up to my Confirmation – the Scouts and Guides paraded their flags and filed into church in their uniforms two by two. Soon I was a Brownie, and later a Girl Guide, although by twelve I just used the experience as a way of getting badges and more certificates, in everything from knot-tying to map-reading. It all appealed to my competitive spirit, although even at that age it was obvious I wasn't really a team player. I only went camping once, to Epping Forest, and found the experience of sharing a tent with three other girls a damp and depressing one. Queuing up for the toilet block, washing with little metal bowls of lukewarm water, eating overcooked sausages and baked beans were all experiences I vowed never to repeat.

Sundays changed for ever in 1956 when Dad bought an old black-and-white television in a large wooden cabinet. From then on, we didn't bother with the radio serials after tea and the ritual of our Sunday bath when we were given use of the lodger's bathroom. Now we would sit around the kitchen table glued to Liberace thrashing around at his piano with a candelabra on top, followed by *Sunday Night at the London Palladium* if it was not term time.

On Saturday mornings I used go to the cinema at the ABC Regal in Fulham Broadway, proudly sporting my ABC Minors badge. But because Fulham kids were so noisy and boisterous, the manager was forever stopping the film and leaping on the stage to bollock us for chucking ice-creams at the screen or running up and down the aisles. I wore special cardboard glasses for 3-D shorts filmed at the Battersea Fun Fair. Girls would be dashing to the lavatories to be sick if they'd eaten too many sweets before the big dipper sequences when we'd all scream our heads off in terror. I don't think I ever saw an episode of the Lone Ranger all the way through. I used to emerge blinking into the sunlight at 12 o'clock, and sometimes my parents and Pat would meet me and we'd go to the pie and mash shop in North End Road. Ugh! I would never eat that muck. I preferred to hang out in Barbers in North End Road – my favourite department store. In fact, till I was ten it was the only department store I'd ever been to, occupying a whole block in the busy street market and offering an oasis of calm from the shouting and jostling around the fruit and vegetable stalls outside. Crammed into two floors were departments for haberdashery and drapery, men's and women's fashions, shoes, home furnishings and kitchen-ware. At Christmas we would queue to visit Santa in his grotto.

Barbers had a polished green linoleum floor, wooden staircases, and an arcane system for taking your cash. I loved the moments after my mother made a purchase, when the assistant would write out a receipt, tear off two copies which he would place with her money in a glass and metal tube, push it into a hole and pull a lever. It would whoosh off and then, a couple of agonising minutes later, another tube would whiz back, which would be ceremoniously opened to reveal our copy of the receipt and her change. Where did these tubes go? Mum would never tell me. I imagined a grotto, like Santa's, under the store full of clerks in black suits with starchy white collars sitting at long desks counting out money and issuing receipts, a bit like something out of a Charles Dickens novel. Barbers closed eventually without me ever finding out.

My sister and I enjoyed going swimming at the Fulham Baths in the Broadway every week. We'd end our sessions with mugs of hot Bovril in the cafe off the entrance. Before long, we'd got certificates signed by the Mayor confirming we'd achieved ten yards, then twenty-five yards unaided, to add to our growing collection of awards. Swimming was great – you didn't have to talk to anyone, and you could plough up and down racking up more and more lengths. Then, to our acute embarrassment, Mum announced that she too was joining us and learning to swim! The complete bloody horrible shame of it!

The shallow end of the pool was roped off for lessons and slung across it was a pulley system, from which dangled a large black-rubber harness. Normally little kids strapped this on and flapped their arms about as they tried to make it across the pool. Now our giant (so it seemed to us) mother crammed herself into this contraption, wearing a rather glamorous one-piece bathing suit and rubber hat, simpering in the direction of the burly male teacher who started bellowing instructions at her to move her arms in a circular fashion and kick her feet. She seemed to be making a complete bloody attention-seeking meal of it to me, as I ploughed up and down at the deep end wishing she would bog off. She'd grown up in a seaside village but never gone swimming, and was belatedly determined to learn. After a month of lessons and a lot of arm flapping, she did a width of ten yards and then after another month, she struggled all the way to the end of the pool, and got her own certificate signed by the Mayor, somewhat diminishing our achievement, it seemed to us. My sister and I

refused to be thwarted, spending more and more time ploughing up and down that pool, racking up the lengths. I called it a day after I'd swum a mile and a half, hundred of lengths, but my sister went on to do two miles and swim at championship level. Mum wisely gave up her lessons and took to ferrying my sister to competitions.

Every day I would walk the length of Parsons Green Lane to Peterborough Primary School, clutching my thin over-coat around me against the winter winds. Soon I had nasty red patches above my knees where the serge of my gymslip had rubbed. In spite of being taunted because of my height and my horrible National Health specs, I enjoyed junior school and my lessons, although the music teacher was extremely frightening and would whack the back of your legs with a ruler if you didn't hit the notes in choir practice. Even though I had virtually no sense of pitch, I was singing in the school choir at a competition in Fulham Town Hall. John Ritz, a boy in the junior school I had a bit of a crush on, took me to see Handel's *Messiah* at a church in Putney, but all we did was hold hands.

Soon, all those lonely hours of scratching away with a pen in detention finally paid off, and I sat the Eleven-plus examination using a pen along with the rest of my class. In the summer of 1958, my parents were thrilled that I had passed it, as well as winning an art prize at school, and they applied for me to attend the establishment I had walked past every day on my way to Peterborough: Lady Margaret's Church of England Grammar School for Girls, on Parsons Green. My classmates filled my autograph book with their good wishes, and Miss Perry my form mistress piously wrote:

3

Jellyfish and Rain

OVER THE BACK door of the whitewashed stone cottage were two nails, about a foot apart, set at the same height. My sister and I stopped in the yard, next to the ancient rusting mangle, which was covered with an oilcloth. We looked up. My Welsh granny, a short, stooped lady with grey hair fastened back in a bun at her neck, was positioned between us and the entrance to the house. 'See that,' she said, pointing at what lay resting on the nails. We nodded silently. Nain was not someone to be messed with. Her command of English might have been minimal, her breathing laboured and bronchial, and she was never seen without an apron and battered slippers, but she never let us forget just who was the boss here.

We had just been deposited at Llwyn Ysgaw, her cottage up the hill at the back of Llanfairfechan, by Gareth Taxi, after a short drive from the station. This was the ritual beginning to any holiday in Wales: the inspection and acknowledgement of the freshly made birch rod. A slim bundle of twigs, stripped of their leaves, had been bound with red button thread and one end given an extra binding of white string to form a handle. 'Any trouble, girls, and you know what you're in for, then,' she stated firmly.

'Yes, Nain,' we chorused in polite reply.

Formalities over, we tucked into high tea of thick slices of toast and poached eggs, buttered *bara brith* (fruit bread) and mugs of tea poured from a metal pot, sitting around the three sides of a table covered with oilcloth in the scullery that had been tacked on to the back of her two-up two-down cottage. The toilet was across the yard, past the mangle, in a stone shed with a corrugated tin roof which also contained the coal store. Freezing cold and unwelcoming in all seasons, it was part of the Llanfairfechan experience. In the whitewashed high stone wall between her enclosed yard and her neighbour's was a large square hole at head height, so Nain could chat to Mrs Russell whenever she wanted. Inside, the small and dark front room was filled by a sofa and an easy chair covered with thick-cut velvet cloths, a loud-ticking grandfather clock, and her proudest possession of all, a large, framed reproduction of 'Bubbles' by Millais. There was a rag rug in front of the grate and a pair of exceeding ugly cream and black Staffordshire dogs on the mantelpiece above it. One wall of the room was dominated by a large dark-oak wooden dresser with brass handles, on which were ranged a set of her best china, patterned Mason's Ironstone plates in all sizes from dessert to meat plates. The door at the front of the house was never opened in my memory, and draughts were excluded with a thick dark curtain over it, hanging from a brass rail. The locals claimed that the only time people went through their front doors was in their coffins, and all visitors would walk around the side of the house and through the yard to the back door. In the cupboard set in the wall by the fire were some toys, a beautifully decorated set of building blocks with pictures pasted on each side, a book about a chow dog's trip to a royal coronation and another about a young girl's visions of the Virgin Mary at Lourdes, which I must have read three years running in the absence of any other reading material in English.

The back room downstairs had a couple of wooden armchairs either side of a black metal range, where a kettle was suspended on a hook and a fire burned throughout the year. Another of Nain's prized knick-knacks stood on the mantelpiece: a large, nasty, mustard-coloured china cat, with a china bandage around its jaw. 'Toothache,' my mother once informed me, as if that explained its significance. Up the steep, dark wooden stairs from this room lay the two bedrooms, each containing a large double bed with Victorian mahogany head and end boards and sagging feather mattresses. To enter the front room where Nain slept, you walked through the back room, where my sister and I would share the bed. A large picture of Jesus was at the top of the stairs, watching over us. The beds were covered with brightly coloured crochet blankets Nain had made from leftover scraps of wool.

Not only was Llanfairfechan a long train journey from Euston via Crewe and Llandudno junction, on a train that would eventually disgorge people at the Holyhead ferry to Ireland in Anglesey, but it represented a totally alien world to us city dwellers. Nain had spent nearly all her life here, and my mother and all her sisters had spent their childhood here living in rented stone cottages, in this small village, which threaded up a valley either side of a river all the way from the beach and the end of the Menai Straits to the volcanic slopes of Mount Dinas at the foot of the mountains behind. They were intimately acquainted with the genealogy and personal habits of every local inhabitant and seemed to be able to recall events of twenty and thirty years ago as if they were yesterday. Not only did they imbue every local landmark with a story or anecdote each time we went for a walk — as in 'See, there, that's where Cinderella Jones was found in her nightie that night after the war . . .' or, 'That's the stone your uncle used to slide down every day on the way to school' — but the very repetition of these mantras served to reinforce their sense of belonging. Unfortunately, it only helped make my sister and me feel even more like intruders or foreigners, people who didn't speak the language and didn't really belong.

We had got used to having Welsh spoken in our house daily in Fulham, but that was nothing compared to our endless weeks in Llanfairfechan. For a start, Welsh was my nain's first language and she used it completely naturally when talking to any of her family. Most of the people in the village were the same, and shopping was a nightmare of incomprehensible jabbering: we would spend hours sitting bored on a couple of wooden chairs by the counter in the Co-op while my mother would have a lengthy chat in Welsh with every new customer as well as the salesman, before finally opting for six slices of bacon and a packet of tea. It was considered rude not to enquire after everyone's health and, as my mother only came home every six months or so, going through these niceties would take hours of each day. The hour in the Co-op would be followed by a lengthy chat in Spiers the bakery and Hinchcliffes the newsagents, which was tantalisingly situated on the final stretch of the road down to the beach. We'd then turn around and slog all the way back up the hill to Llwyn Ysgaw for lunch of a slice of ham and salad, or mashed potato and sausage. Then, if the weather was fine, Pat, Mum and I would walk all the way back down, under the railway bridge, past Moranedd, the grand Victorian house with its charming circular tower and pointed turret, where Nain used to work, on the seafront opposite the large timbered cafe. Then we'd turn left, past the model yacht pond, and head along the Cob for a short stroll before flopping out in the grass behind the sea wall for a spot of sunbathing. There was a bus service that ran regularly up and down the village, from the beach cafe to the place at the top of the village where the rivers met called Three Streams, but as we never had any spare cash for public transport we never used it.

Nearly all my school holidays over a ten-year period – Easter, Whitsun and summer – were spent in  Llanfairfechan. For a start, we had no money for fancy hotels or boarding houses, and Nain's house was a cheap option. She adored us and we her, even though she didn't speak much English and was pretty strict about bedtimes and staying out late chatting to local boys. It meant that Mum and Dad could deposit us there and then go back to London and work, although when we were small my mother spent most of the time there with us too. As the train tickets were expensive, and we didn't have a car when I was very small, it made more sense for us to stay up there and my father to just come in one block of two weeks, when Nain would sleep downstairs on a camp bed or next door in her neighbour's house. This annual routine was broken by a couple of holidays in Bournemouth, when we stayed in a flat near Auntie Eileen's relatives and she accompanied us, and one memorable trip to Mevagissey in Cornwall when we'd rented a cottage on the road down to the beach.

By the time I was six my father had acquired the first of his many second-hand cars, a large black Armstrong Siddeley which had been used as some sort of official vehicle. My sister and I were placed in the back, with a large potty, at dawn one August morning. My father treated each holiday as the equivalent of a troop movement, and we had to be packed the night before and have our luggage inspected and loaded. We were roused at dawn and always got underway before breakfast, no later than 6.30 a.m. On this occasion he informed us there were going to be no stops. If we wanted to pee then we had to go in the potty and Mum would chuck it out of the car window while we were moving. I remember hoping that none of the other kids in the street would see me getting into such an embarrassing vehicle. Between dozing in the back, which was like a large playroom to us, my sister and I started doing a jigsaw on the car floor. Soon, we felt violently car sick – but of course Dad would not stop, so we puked in the potty and Mum threw it out when we were going through Devon.

On arrival in Mevagissey, I was thrilled to be released from my confinement and ran down to the beach to play before supper and bed. Next day we woke up and the car was no longer parked outside our cottage. Huge drama! Dad had forgotten to put blocks in front of the wheels (the handbrake was defective) and it had run all the way down the hill, nearly ending up on the beach. Recriminations all round followed, with my mother blaming my father for not getting a decent car and making us a laughing stock. I couldn't see the problem, because we had only just arrived in the village and didn't know anyone anyway! She was probably just cross that he had triumphed and our holiday was being spent somewhere where everyone spoke English.

Mum got her way, and the next year we were back in Wales, this time being driven in a tiny blue Austin A35, a journey of at least seven hours on the narrow and winding A5. The fields changed colour as we drove through the Midlands, then Shropshire, and finally through Llangollen, where they seemed bright green and vibrant. Of course the colour could have had something to do with the plentiful rain. I was delighted when we finally reached the gloomy slate village of Bethesda, where my Welsh granddad had been born, now I knew that Bangor and the end of our journey were not far away.

We were to have many second-hand cars over the years, but my father adored his blue A35, and was distraught when a few months later he found it had been stolen in Fulham. The whole family – Mum, Dad, Auntie Vi pushing Pat, who was about five, in a pushchair, and I – gathered on Putney Bridge, where we stood watch for hours, convinced that the crook would drive past in it. He never did, and we never saw it again.

Without a car, we went to Wales on the train with

Mum when school term ended in July in 1954. By now Uncle Ray had bought a motorbike, with a sidecar, and after we had been away for two weeks he arrived with Dad on the pillion and Auntie Vi in the sidecar. I was so excited to see Uncle Ray, who meant holiday fun, that I ran out of the cottage to meet them and immediately burnt my leg rather badly on the hot exhaust pipe. I couldn't go swimming and had a big white bandage on my leg for the whole of August, just adding to the misery of being in Wales. The next year we made the journey in a second-hand van, with no windows in the back. We had all the usual rituals, the 6.30 a.m. start, no breakfast till we reached somewhere called Brownhills north of Birmingham, where Mum put on an apron and cooked a fry-up of bacon and eggs on a primus stove in a lay-by. Oh, how I longed for a meal in a cafe like other people! The journey up the A5 (no motorways in those days) was as interminable as ever, and my sister was reduced to counting milk churns to pass the hours, while I read till I felt car sick.

Every year when we reached Lake Ogwen in Snowdonia, Dad would be forced to stop the car as the same ritual was re-enacted. Mum would take off her sandals and step over stones into the brown uninviting water, smiling idiotically and saying, 'We're here!' She had told me that Llyn (lake) Ogwen was so deep it couldn't be measured, that it was a magical place where Welsh wizards lived in olden days. Years later I found out that this dark and miserable stretch of water lying in the shadow of Snowdon is just four feet deep. One year it was raining and thundering so badly as we drove up the A5 past Llangollen that my sister was bawling her head off and begging Dad to stop before we got killed. As we approached Bethesda, another ritual started as Mum would whip out her handbag, rummage around for her compact, comb her hair, powder her face and carefully apply lipstick before we entered home terri-tory. She would step from the car looking impossibly glamorous and uncreased, for the full benefit of the neighbours, whereas my sister and I would be covered in spots of sick and bits of chocolate. Appearance was everything in the closed community of Llanfairfechan, and it was important to her that everyone thought she was doing well.

end of the promenade, a huge mountain that had been systematically blasted apart, with a small area still being worked on the top and the dull boom of blasting sounded every day at noon. It looked more or less unchanged since the days in the 1930s when my grandfather had struggled up there to work, crippled by a series of strokes. Below, scree slopes dropped hundreds of feet down to the coastal road, the railway next to it, and the sea. There was no real esplanade, just a stretch of grass, with a garden at one end next to the Crazy Golf and a small terrace of Victorian seaside villas, which had been turned into boarding houses or holiday flats. On the corner of Station Road, which was the route up through the village, was a white, rounded 1930s building which housed a small amusement arcade. That, and the fleapit cinema in the village up the road from the Co-op, were our only sources of entertainment for weeks on end. Nain's brother Uncle Joe in Menai gave me a wooden boat as a present one summer, and I spent hours sailing it on the wooden boating pond, which was always half empty, full of dank, dirty-looking water and a lot of rubbish. On Sundays a handful of enthusiasts would gather and operate their remote-controlled speedboats, which was very noisy and exciting and thoroughly frowned on by the religious fanatics.

At Llanfairfechan the tide literally went out for miles, leaving sand as far as the eye could see, seeming to stretch all the way to the coast of Anglesey and Beaumaris on the other side of the channel. My mother would terrify us about walking on the beach at low tide, claiming there was 'quicksand' and we would be sucked to our deaths. More frightening than the quicksand was the presence of large rubbery things deposited by the outgoing tide at regular intervals. All the largest and most vicious jellyfish in Northern Europe seemed to have decided to congregate on the shore here at Llanfairfechan. Appropriately named, the Portuguese man-of-war jellyfish would deliver an unforgettable sting if you had the misfortune to swim into one. After a couple of hours you were left with a throbbing numbness and a long, raised, red wheal, as if you'd been electrocuted or hit with a cattle prod. No wonder we didn't do a lot of serious water activities – apart from anything else, the weather was generally cold, windy and wet. Summer in North Wales seemed to happen in June, when we were in school, rather than during our actual summer holidays. My sister and I would don horrid ruched swimming costumes and make sandcastles, frequently popping on a cardigan to keep out the stiff breeze. If the sun ever did come out, Mum would slather us in a mixture of cooking oils, as we couldn't afford suntan lotion.

Behind the beach the mountains framed a glorious view. We never ventured further than the woods a couple of hundred yards along the Cob, because behind them lay a secure mental hospital and Mum had put the fear of God into us about talking to anyone who might have come from there. This huge detached Victorian house was where several hundred violent and disturbed souls were looked after, and it was a source of endless speculation and wild rumours in the village. A Victorian bathing hut built for the inmates down by the far end of the Cob with wrought-iron railings and wooden decking over the pebbles lay falling into disrepair, and if we timidly approached it without Mum, my heart would be beating wildly and I was convinced a madman would emerge from the woods and drag us off. Further along the deserted beach lay Shell Island and the coastal path to Aber, but we never dared take it. From time to time we would see people on the beach here accompanied by nurses, but we stayed well away. Nain would collect the twigs from our birch rod from the woods by the mental hospital, or so she told us.

If the beach was a place reputedly frequented by violent lunatics, the mountains behind the village were equally the source of endless stories and myths. Some of these had obviously been told by Nain to my mother and her sisters as children to send them to sleep, or keep them from straying far from home, but by the time I was in Llanfairfechan in the 1950s, they were treated as part of local history, fact and fiction had blended into one. The top of the mountain Drum was where giants lived, and fairies lived in the woods above Three Streams. The little perfectly rounded volcanic hill of Dinas above Three Streams was home to witches, and it was highly dangerous to try and climb it. Immediately behind the village lay the mountain of Carreg Fawr and all around it were standing stones and Neolithic remains. The top of Carreg Fawr was a rocky outcrop, and always looked to me like a face with a long nose and closed eyes, as if a giant was taking a nap. Sheep grazed in the bright green meadows which were surrounded by walls made from reject pieces of slate. The lower slopes of the mountain were covered with a sprinkling of houses and farms, linked by Terrace Walk, a tarmac narrow lane with panoramic views. Climbing up to Terrace Walk from Nain's cottage meant ascending a hundred steep stone steps, with a well-polished metal balustrade for support. But neither my mother or my nain had any concept of going for a walk just for the pleasure of it. Every time we left the house it was carrying a bag, to collect twigs for firewood, blackberries for jam, bilberries

for pies, mushrooms for breakfast. Walking meant foraging. My mother and I would climb beyond Carreg Fawr, to pick bilberries on the moors below the slopes of Drum, which she told me was a cursed mountain, never explaining why.

One Saturday we walked up the river above the cottage to Three Streams, the place where the rivers joined at the foot of Dinas, a local beauty spot. Then we followed a path up on to the top of the moor, heading eventually for Conwy via the remains of the old Roman Road. High up, on a windswept lonely plateau, it began to pour with rain. We crouched behind a wall to shelter, when suddenly, from nowhere it seemed to me, a man appeared and said hello. I couldn't speak, I was absolutely terrified. My mother had told me so many stories about these mountains that I was convinced this man was going to knock us down and rob us. I was literally shaking with fear. My mother accepted a cigarette from him, and they briefly conversed in Welsh while she smoked it. Soon, the rain abated slightly and I said from under my pulled-up rain hood, 'Let's get going!'

'She's in a bit of a hurry,' said the stranger. My mother laughed, enjoying his attention. I could stand it no longer and strode off down the Roman Road in the direction of Conwy and the bus home. Pretty soon she caught up with me. He had headed off in another direction. For that one brief moment in the storm, I got a glimpse of what an incredible flirt my mother must have been. A week later, Dad arrived and we all crammed in the car and headed over to Anglesey for a picnic at Red Wharf Bay near Benllech (with Violet, Ray and Pat). As Mum fiddled with the primus stove and Dad gazed off into the distance with his binoculars, I noted that she was wearing a daring off-the-shoulder blouse and a string of pearls. Who was she hoping to impress?

My final summer in Wales was in 1961, where I spent two evenings a week at the cinema in the village or in Bangor, so bored I watched *GI Blues* around twice. I hung out with my cousin John, Auntie Phyllis's son, and my cousin Jennifer who was Poprin's eldest daughter, visiting from Manchester. Asked on a date by Gwylem, a local lad, who I'd met by hanging around the amusement arcade, I stood him up and went and watched my first X-film, *Faces in the Dark*, by myself in the fleapit village cinema instead. Much more exciting than drinking beer and being groped down on the Cob. I couldn't wait to get back to London and spend hours hanging out at the annual funfair on the edge of Wimbledon Common.

The following year, in an effort to ring the changes, Dad decided to try spending a different kind of family holiday, a weekend in a caravan outside Aldeburgh in Suffolk. We left Fulham at 6.15 a.m. one Saturday in June, packed and inspected as per usual. That evening, in a field next to the caravan park, he decided, totally out of character, to try and teach me how to drive. It was the first and last time. I put our old Ford into gear, but got confused and we ended up in a hedge with Dad red-faced and screaming at me. Luckily no damage was done, and the incident forgotten. I gave up all attempts to drive until twenty years later, and have never been in a caravan since – the sense of claustrophobia and lack of privacy of that weekend is too powerful a memory. Four tall, difficult

4

Sickness and Spells

I LAY IN MY bed at Elmstone Road shivering and sweating. Across the room I could make out the shape of my sister lying silently. It was a weekday morning but neither of us was about to get up and get dressed for school. I had no sense of time. After a while – it could have been one or three hours as I drifted in and out of consciousness – my mother and father entered the room. She leant over me and said softly, 'Don't worry, you're going to be going somewhere where you'll get better.' I said nothing in reply, I was feeling too weak. For days my sister and I had been sick with bad stomach cramps and severe diarrhoea. Eating was impossible. All I could drink was water, and even that made me feel nauseous.

I was aware of being wrapped in blankets like a parcel, and being hoisted over my father's shoulder. My mother picked up my sister behind me. I felt each step as we slowly went down the stairs into the hall, and then my father turned – not towards the front door, but back, towards the kitchen and the scullery. 'What's happening?' I muttered and got no answer. He took me through the kitchen, where the fire was burning in the grate, through the narrow scullery, past the kitchen sink, with the plates from lunch stacked up to dry in the rack. We were in the back garden. I couldn't understand where I was going, felt frightened and cried out in confusion, only to be told by my mother, 'Shh, shh, it will all be all right . . .'

I was lifted up and passed over the wall at the rear of our garden, into a neighbour's backyard. There, an unfamiliar man took hold of me, and I started to snivel. He pushed the blankets tighter together around me and quickly took me through their ground floor, out through the hall, over the pavement outside 23 Harbledown Road and into the back of a vehicle, where I was strapped into a bunk bed. My sister, also crying, joined me on the opposite bunk. We were in an ambulance – our first ever, and on our way to hospital, where we would remain for the next six weeks, suffering from amoebic dysentery. My mother, for reasons known only to her, had decided that if the ambulance drew up outside our house, then neighbours would think she was deficient in some aspect of parenting. And so she had told it to wait in the next road and my sister and I were handed over garden walls like a couple of prizes in a game of pass the parcel. We were six and four years old.

This was probably the first time that I realised my mother was rather odd, and I had ample time to think about her behaviour during the lonely weeks we spent in a large Victorian hospital in a distant and unfamiliar northern suburb of London under close surveillance. My sister and I had to use bedpans and their contents were meticulously analysed. Our temperatures were taken every few hours and filled in on charts that hung on the metal rail at the end of our beds. After a while – I have no idea how many days or weeks as the regime all blended into one – we gradually stopped feeling weak and started eating again, albeit on a diet that seemed white and colourless: broth, rice, steamed chicken. No one ever discovered how we got sick or, if they did know, nobody bothered to tell us. After six weeks Dad collected us and we returned to home and school and our normal routine.

There was to be a regular pattern established at home, that unpleasant things simply weren't discussed or referred to again, and that extended to everything from my parents' non-marriage to illness of any description. Another taboo subject was death and burials, and when any relatives died either in Llanfairfechan or London, my sister and I were never taken to the funerals. When our granddad died, even though we had both enjoyed his company on our visits to Southgate, it was not thought a good idea for us to attend his funeral or the wake. Both my parents had the unfortunate habit of airbrushing difficult things out of their (and our) lives.

My sister and I soon became an accident-prone pair. One day after school, I went to Hurlingham Park, near the river, after school to play. Running after a ball along an asphalt path I tripped and fell on to a short iron stake on the edge of the grass. It pierced my skinny, stick-like right leg and I fell on the ground, screaming in agony.

quickly took it off and used it as our third base. Sadly, I had placed it on a pile of fresh dog shit, and at the end of the game at 8 o'clock, when I lifted my new cardigan up to go home, it was encrusted with brown foul-smelling stains. Back at Elmstone Road, my mother was furious, and slapped me – as if I'd done it on purpose! I refused to wear the offending garment again, even when she'd washed it. As far as I was concerned, it was cursed.

Both parents were extremely concerned with what our neighbours thought, and would go to extraordinary lengths not to do anything that might draw attention to our household. Sometimes the result was just plain ludicrous. Tall and slim, Pat and I had virtually no sense of balance. She tripped in Parsons Green Lane on her way home from primary school and hit her head on the polished granite of a pub entrance. A massive cut over her eyebrow resulted – luckily she didn't need stitches. Then, one Saturday morning I was playing my favourite game in the street outside our house, called London to Paris, which involved hopping up and down a chalked ladder kicking a stone. As I leapt from behind two parked cars a motorbike hit me sideways and my chin got rammed upwards by the handlebars. Having large frilly teeth, even at ten, meant that my top teeth got firmly embedded in my bottom lip, which started bleeding profusely. A kid banged on our front door and my mother soon came out and went ballistic. We didn't have a telephone, but there was no question of calling for an ambulance — that would have alerted the neighbours to my plight.

Darting back indoors, she reappeared on the pavement where I lay whimpering with a handful of clean tea towels, quickly swathed my head with them, jammed my arms through the sleeves of my school raincoat and dragged me, protesting and crying, up the road behind her, to the 28 bus stop on Fulham Road. I was nearly unconscious with the pain, and could hardly see anything through the makeshift bandages. After a couple of minutes I silently thanked God as the bus came and Mum bundled me on the lower deck and told me to keep quiet. She bought two tickets to St Stephen's Hospital, a ten-minute journey, and when a fellow passenger, a kindly middle-aged lady, asked what had happened to the little girl, my mother said, 'Nothing, she's just had a bit of a tumble.'

At our stop I was bundled off the bus, across the road

and through the familiar portals of Casualty. My mother marched up to the counter and told them I'd had a slight accident. By then blood was seeping through my Invisible Man disguise and I must have looked a frightening sight as we were rapidly whisked into a cubicle. When the doctor arrived and started carefully unpeeling the tea towels, my mother immediately passed out and hit her head on the floor. I was mopped up, given various tetanus shots and had the gash across my lower lip stitched up. We got a lift home in an ambulance, but, fearful of the neighbours, my mother made it stop around the corner and we walked the final fifty yards. Once in the front door, my father started laying into me about not taking care when playing, not looking out for traffic, causing them endless worry and so on. I had to eat liquid food for a couple of weeks through a straw, so I guess that was even more trouble for them. My lip healed but still felt lumpy and I was left with a long fine scar and an even more sulky expression.

While my mother hated hospitals (perhaps under-standably), she had a strong belief in the power of spells and magic; I don't know if it was stuff her mother taught her when she was growing up in Wales or not. Every Sunday, when my sister and I came home from Sunday School, we would have high tea at 5 p.m. – a tin of ham or tongue, hard-boiled eggs, a lettuce, tomatoes, salad cream, spring onions, beetroot, and slices of white bread. A home-made sponge cake and a large pot of tea, and then my mother would inspect all the tea leaves at the bottom of our cups and try and tell our fortunes for the weeks ahead. It was an entertaining diversion, followed by a wash in the tin bath in the kitchen in front of the fire, while listening to *Journey into Space* on the radio. This long-running drama serial used to scare the living daylights out of me, the sound effects were so good: endless whistling winds while the spaceship was grounded on Mars – and I would frequently wake up after a couple of hours' sleep shivering and shaking from a nightmare in which I was stuck on a distant planet with alien monsters approaching my spacecraft.

Another tea-time diversion was my mother's unique approach to any skin blemish, be it a wart, a lump or whatever. She would cut a potato in half and chant some Welsh mumbo-jumbo while she rubbed the cut half on the offending bit of flesh. Then she would make a bandage from ripped-up strips of old sheets and tie it over the affected part. We would then go out into the back garden where a small hole was dug and the half of the potato solemnly buried, accompanied by more Welsh chanting. We were ordered to keep the bandage on for a week, and next Sunday at the same time we would look for the potato in the garden. It had invariably disappeared (maybe she hid it) and she would announce triumphantly: 'That means the wart has gone too!' There would be a ceremonial unwrapping of the (by now) filthy grey bandage, and hey presto! No wart! I don't know how she did it, but it certainly seemed to work.

Both my sister and I hated the dentist. When very young I went to one in Fulham, but when I regained consciousness after being given gas for an extraction, I felt sure that my clothes had been rearranged somehow. When I bravely told Mum that I thought the dentist was touching me, she just clipped me around the ear and told me not to be stupid. I refused to go to his surgery again, and so she found another dentist near Parsons Green. This man seemed to inflict unnecessary suffering, and used the drill endlessly. I screamed the place down, biting him on several occasions. In the end my teeth were so poorly looked after that when I was about twelve the whole of one summer holiday in North Wales was taken up with daily trips to the dentist in Colwyn Bay — I must have had ten fillings in a week.

The dentist wasn't the first time I felt unwanted attention from a middle-aged man. When I was about eight, my sister and I were taken to an old-fashioned hairdresser's. My mother left me there to have my hair cut for the new school term while she popped to the dairy further down the road, run by some fellow Welsh speakers.

I will never forget what happened during the fifteen minutes or so I was alone with the hairdresser. A middle-aged portly chap with Brylcreemed hair, he showed me into a wooden panelled cubicle, placed a couple of cushions on the chair to raise me up, and then draped a robe around my shoulders, stroking it over my chest in a rather disturbing way as if to flatten and smooth out the fabric. I focused on a couple of tulips drooping in a vase on the counter in front of the Art Deco mirror. He carefully cut my hair in a very severe and unflattering bob, occasionally letting his hands drop and touch my neck and chest. I sat frozen in front of my image in the mirror, unable to speak — it was as if I was moving in slow motion in a dream. Eventually my mother returned with some shopping, pronounced the horrible haircut a great success — 'very nice and tidy' — paid at the cash till on the glass counter at the front of the shop and told me to say goodbye politely. After tea, when I told her I wouldn't ever go there again, she just told me to shut up and not be stupid. And I couldn't tell her why because she would never have believed me, and might even have given me a bash with the hairbrush for 'telling stupid stories'. But luckily my next visit a month later passed off without incident and the groping never happened again; maybe my tormentor moved on to some other unsuspecting young girl with prettier hair.

The fact Mum had refused to believe my stories about inappropriate adult behaviour just confirmed in my mind that she wasn't really on my side in life. She had this tendency to treat me as if I was a nuisance, a story-teller or fantasist, a self-centred junior troublemaker. And so subtly, over the years, our relationship was defined, her on one side against me on the other.

A few years later, my mother decided that my feet were too big. They were large for my age, admittedly, about a size 8, but it was the lumps on the bones of my heels that were a problem. She decided to consult the local doctor, who told her that it would be possible to cut away these 'spurs' and make it easier to find shoes to fit me. By now I was commuting miles across London to grammar school, and studying for exams, but she still thought it important I should have the operation. After endless Outpatients appointments in Acton, I was eventually admitted to a hospital in Harrow and the operation was performed, leaving long scars around the back of each heel. It took a full two weeks to convalesce and I returned home on crutches wearing flipflop sandals, as my feet were covered in thick bandages. I was pretty excited at the possibility of having glamorous feet, and couldn't wait for the unveiling a month later. Sadly, the operation was a complete failure. From then on, any pair of new shoes would send the scar tissue into a swollen mass of red blisters, and I was no better off than before. That would be my last real trip to a hospital as an in-patient for twenty years – I'd had enough of them by the time I was a teenager. And as for my teeth sticking out: I told my mother that there was no way I would ever wear braces, I would be visiting the dentist as little as possible in future. My sister, on the other hand, dutifully submitted and spent the next two years with a mouth full of metal.

One night I screamed my head off sitting in the cobwebby darkness of our outside toilet as a large frog jumped over my right foot. Robert Knapp had been up to his tricks again. Robert's home in Harbledown Road backed on to ours, and his mother Sylvia was not only one of my mother's best friends, she was also my sister's godmother. Robert was exactly the same age as my sister, and his sister Juana was the same age as me. There was another younger girl, Barbara. We were in and out of each other's houses all the time, noisy kids who liked fancy dress, would play in the street and go on outings on the weekends in the summer to the south coast with other friends like John Ritz from Peterborough Junior School.

We would go to Richmond Park after school every spring and collect frog spawn from Pen Ponds in jamjars, keeping them on the windowsills in our backyards, eventually returning them to their natural home in the wilderness of the ponds when they grew little arms and legs. Clearly Robert had kept his booty and now this frog was another of the little ways he could use to taunt us.

I loved the whole process of collecting the slimy jelly and watching it gradually turn into little wriggling things in water, preferring reptiles and non-communicative fish to most pets, particularly fluffy cats and dogs and our Welsh-speaking budgerigar, Nicky. I decided to go one step further and build a version of Pen Ponds in our own back garden, in a corner opposite our one tree, a dreary orange blossom. I used leftover bits of rubble from building sites to make a mini rockery setting, collecting them on my way home from school in my satchel. The pond itself was made from a rusty tin bowl my mother had discarded. In it I put a terrapin purchased at the pet shop in North End Road. For a couple of months my pond was the talk of the street, and the Knapp kids were full of admiration. Then one day I rushed home from school to discover Terry the terrapin was dead, probably mauled by a neighbour's cat, according to my mother. He was just lying on his back, little legs limp and lifeless, head flopping to one side. No sign of blood. Personally, I didn't go for the killer cat theory and suspected foul play on the part of a jealous Robert Knapp, but could prove nothing. (Perhaps this was an omen of his future career, which has now ended with a life sentence for murder.)

I was distraught. The terrapin was solemnly wrapped in tissue and put in a Barbers' brown paper bag, and we held a burial ceremony during which my mother said some Welsh prayers. Terry the terrapin was interred under the orange-blossom tree and I made a little tombstone by scratching his name on a piece of slate I'd brought home from North Wales the previous summer. A few years later Nicky the budgie was found feet-up in the bottom of his cage and another funeral service re-enacted, this time with slightly more Welsh. Frankly my sister and I weren't so bothered about the irritating budgie, but my mother took his demise quite badly. Now there were two little purple slate tombstones in our pet cemetery.

We were all exhuberant noisy kids, but Robert seemed to play that bit harder than the rest of us. One day he hit my sister over the head with a brick – and when she complained to my mother, the result was terrifying. She confronted Robert's father Arthur who beat him so badly with a belt my sister couldn't stop crying. Robert's family were better off than ours, occupying a whole house, and his father Arthur was a Clerk of the Works. Arthur seemed a menacing, unfriendly character — we believed he was some kind of mysterious secret member of the police reserves — and his mother was a sweet, soft, trusting person totally in his thrall.

I wasn't surprised Robert Knapp clouted my sister with a brick — she could be very irritating. Robert was an attractive, lively boy, really smart and full of fun. But he had a nasty side as well, and we took great care not to annoy him after the brick incident. Our group played rounders together on Parsons Green and Eel Brook Common after school. We would dress up as cowboys and cowgirls at Christmas and go to other children's parties together while we were all still at primary school. I soon acquired, like Robert, a fearsome reputation for bad behaviour on these occasions. I couldn't understand why it was not a party for me personally, and would frequently open all the presents for the birthday boy or girl, which would inevitably end up with my mother giving me a good clip around the head. Undeterred, I would eat as much jelly and cake as I could, cheat at pass the parcel and musical chairs, and leave in disgrace, never to be invited back again.

One day my mother took me to a party for another
eight-year-old near the Wandsworth Bridge Road. It must
have been January, because I was wearing new black
patent-leather shoes with a bar across that I'd been given
for Christmas. On the way home, dragging me down

Parsons Green Lane, Mum was reprimanding me for my self-centred horrible behaviour which she was so ashamed of, when I was violently sick all over my new shoes and white socks. On arriving at Elmstone Road, I was sent to bed in disgrace.

In the late 1950s Fulham was home to plenty of low-level criminals, and not a week passed without the front page of the *Fulham Chronicle* recording a bank hold-up or a robbery with violence. In consecutive weeks of 1957 three shops in the area, including the local branches of Sainsbury's and the Co-op, had their safes blown up with gelignite and considerable sums of money stolen. In August 1963 Fulham hit the headlines again when a mail train was held up in Buckinghamshire and £2,600,000 was stolen. The gang that carried out the Great Train Robbery, as it was soon known, included a William Boal from Fulham, who had rented a garage and bought a used car in Bournemouth to use in the raid. Boal and his wife were charged with receiving stolen goods, hundreds of thousands of pounds, and Boal, who already had three previous convictions, was sentenced to twenty-four years' imprisonment. His wife was acquitted. There were endless reports of youths in 'Edwardian' (i.e. teddy boy) clothing holding up local post offices or simply demanding money with menaces from the fishmongers in North End Road or the local sub-post office. Robert began to hang out with some of these more undesirable elements, leaving us girls alone.

In spite of his reputation, Robert was a stunner by his teens, and very attractive to local girls. At eleven my sister went on to Carlyle Grammar School on the Fulham Road and Robert attended Sloane Boys School next door. By then my Welsh granny had moved down to London to avoid the harsh winters in Snowdonia, as she increasingly suffered from bronchitis, and a room was rented for her on the ground floor of the Knapps' house. She soon complained that she was 'mislaying' money, but we put it down to her forgetfulness at seventy-four. Robert might have been the culprit. He was caught stealing the school dinner money at his junior school only six months after arriving there. To be honest, we were all pretty impressed. Robert Knapp seemed amazingly confident and stylish.

By the time I went to Lady Margaret's Grammar School in 1958, I saw a lot less of Robert and his sister Juana.

5

Your Whole Life Lies Before You . . .

> "Your whole life lies before you,
> like a sheet of driven snow,
> Be careful how you tread it,
> for every mark will show,"
>
> Mummy.
> 11/8/1958

I SLUMPED ON MY bed in the room I shared with my sister in Elmstone Road and looked at her closely out of the corner of my eye. She lay on her bed, quietly, harmlessly, engrossed in a book. I bloody loathed her. For a start she had a sunny, smiley disposition, everyone thought she was really good fun, and she was a jolly tomboy, always willing to play games with the other kids in our street even if it meant getting into trouble. At thirteen I was a moody cow. My sister had dark, shiny hair, whereas mine had darkened from the blonde of my childhood to a dreary, limp, mousy beige. My mother would sometimes twist it and tie it up in strips of rags torn from old sheets, and make me sleep with these horrible lumps in my head. In the morning they would be ceremoniously unfurled and all I would have to show for seven hours' sleep deprivation would be the slightest of kinks at irregular intervals. I would spend hours sitting at the back of the class in Latin or Maths, surreptitiously rubbing toothpaste into my hair (the brands that advertised 'with added peroxide') in the hope of achiev-ing blonde streaks without dye. My hair remained straight and mousy, and now was unattractively matted from the toothpaste.

My sister and I had grown up barely tolerating each other. As the elder, I resented her presence anyway, and we had separate friends from the moment she attended Peterborough Primary School two years after me. We had a kind of wary co-existence, keeping out of each other's way, a relationship in which she had to pretend to me that I was the superior being, even though secretly I suspected she loathed me. We shared a bedroom but we were two very different personalities. My sister was highly intelligent, but for some reason my father treated her as if I was the brainy one, which was very unfair, and she always felt that she had to emulate my good marks at school. I was held up as a role model for her to despise. My father, for example, definitely favoured me as his quasi-son substitute, whereas my mother would always take Pat's side in any dispute.

But today something was different about Pat, she definitely had a new ring of confidence about her. God knows, I was totally self-conscious and insecure about my appearance. Not only did I have periods, uninteresting, unfashionable, beige hair, horrible National Health pink spectacles, big sticking-out front teeth and the longest, thinnest legs at school — as well as no boy-friend — I also had a completely flat chest. Pat, on the other hand, seemed to have sprouted a couple of slight swellings in the breast department. How dare

she, I fumed, and I secretly resolved to kill her as soon as I could.

I had already drawn a line down the middle of our bedroom with chalk and told my sister that if she crossed it she would be 'dead meat'. She would remain cowed and terrified on her bed each night, too scared to go down the stairs to the toilet in the back garden, too scared to use the potty under her bed, placed there for emergencies. Too scared to fall asleep in case she might sleepwalk and be punished by me. She was so frightened of dropping off and moving about in her dreams she used to tie her foot to the bottom of her bed and risk wetting the mattress in her sleep. I showed no mercy, and ruled our bedroom with frequent withering looks calculated to scare the living daylights out of her. I am not entirely sure that I wished her life to be exactly 'snuffed out', but I definitely intended to show that bitch a lesson for growing breasts before me. For weeks now I had gone to bed every night and silently prayed to God to give me tits, but nothing had happened. So, I chose my moment with care, waiting until she was at the top of the stairs outside our bedroom door one morning, poised, with her school uniform on and her satchel on her back, ready to start her trip to school. Without any warning I rushed up behind her and whacked her in the small of her back with all my might. Her legs gave way and she screamed in terror, falling down the whole set of stairs, rolling over in the hall and gashing her forehead on the back of the letterbox. Result! Not entirely as I had hoped, but enough of a frightener to show her who was boss.

My mother rushed out of the kitchen, seized her in her arms and started shouting and crying, carting my sobbing sister off to the scullery to be cleaned up with a clean tea towel. My father appeared and ordered me back into my bedroom from my vantage point at the very spot where I'd started her on her death fall. 'DID YOU PUSH YOUR SISTER?' he bellowed at me. 'Course not,' I simpered back, but it cut no ice with the boss. He hit me really hard on the legs, and then I started a little snivel, just to keep my sister company. Two weeks later I repeated my thump-in-the-back routine, but by now I suspected that my sister was both ready and prepared for my attack. Maybe she'd been watching Saturday afternoon wrestling on television, I don't know, but this time she seemed to be able to slow her fall down and she cleverly rolled over in the hall and got up, giving me the V sign as she pranced out of the front door. I was in total despair. I had to escape from the prison that was life with my family, how I didn't yet know.

I had very reluctantly come to accept that I was my mother's daughter. For years I had hoped that she had picked up the wrong baby in the nursing home and that my real parents would turn up in Fulham to collect me. I imagined they lived in a detached villa in Epsom, Surrey (somewhere I'd never been, but I secretly imagined it was green and middle-class, not street after street of terraced houses full of rough kids like Fulham). My real parents were well-educated professionals (lawyers or teachers) who read the *Guardian* over breakfast and listened to chamber music on the radio in the evening. They ate in a dining room and had intelligent conversations about music, politics and foreign countries. Not like my pretend parents who read the *Daily Mirror* during the week and the *Reynolds News* (the newspaper run by the Co-operative Movement) on Sundays, listened to

Two-Way Family Favourites and the Glums with Jimmy Edwards on our radio on Sundays, and could barely manage a conversation with each other about anything other than our next trip to Wales or to my grim Nana Bull in Southgate. My parents' one bookcase was full of my dad's lurid paperbacks about Japanese atrocities in the Second World War and well-thumbed copies of *Reader's Digest*, as well as various sloppy (in my opinion) Daphne du Maurier novels belonging to Mum.

I was a fully formed snob who observed these people avidly each day as if they were endangered species in a zoo, cringing at each imagined shortcoming on their part. Any rare visits to us by my father's mother (Nana) were extra ammunition. She rarely spoke to my mother and could be guaranteed to vomit back up any meal eaten in our kitchen within thirty minutes of consuming it. She was a thin-lipped woman with a severe bob haircut and a strong sense of order and correctness. Tea at her house in Southgate was a trial, enlivened only by Granddad, who would let us play in the large garden and do a bit of weeding or lounging around in deckchairs reading all his old copies of science magazines. Nana's domain, the kitchen, had a bleak, cheerless quality, every surface ruthlessly scrubbed and cleaned and smelling slightly of the horrible sterilised milk she drank. Tea, when a white cloth was laid over the thick velvet cloth on the circular mahogany table, was a silent affair. No personal touch was evident in the spread she laid out – small bowls of tinned tongue, ruthlessly quartered tomatoes, jars of chutney and salad cream, a bowl of lettuce, a plate of sliced white bread and an opened can of potato salad. I couldn't remember a time when she laughed or seemed enthusiastic, the life seemed to have been scrubbed out of her.

By the time I was thirteen our doorbell had still not been rung by my fantasy parents and so I begrudgingly accepted that the couple who shared a bedroom on the ground floor of our house were in fact my mum and dad. I couldn't imagine them having sex, and my nana was so repulsive I could not countenance that my blood and hers were somehow linked, but in my heart I knew that my mother had actually spawned me. It didn't make me like her any more, however.

I took to hanging out in the Fulham Library at the end

of our road, helping in the children's section after school. As well as being another bolt-hole away from the claustrophobia of 18 Elmstone Road, it meant I could read all the new stuff first, as well as getting my hands on the books in the adult section that you had to put your name on a list for. I moved from Biggles and Jules Verne to D.H. Lawrence within a year, and joined the library quiz team just to keep myself busy. Over the next three years I would join the Young Socialists and the Young Conservatives at the same time, overlapping my membership in both. I had zero interest in party politics, but I was a compulsive competitor and served in the quiz teams of both organisations. The YS group had poetry evenings and wine and cheese parties in a Victorian house off Putney Hill, while the Young Conservatives used to meet in a rather dingy school hall near Hurlingham Park. I made no friends in either group, treating each an exercise in strategy and gamesmanship.

My being accepted by Lady Margaret's School pleased my father no end. He had grown up seeing this snobby girls' school every day as he attended the extremely working-class Holman Hunt Junior School around the corner in New King's Road. He loved the look of the young ladies in their formal uniform of panama hats, gingham shirt-waisted dresses and striped red and black blazers in summer, hexagonal berets, black and red striped scarves and navy coats in winter. It represented a step up for a working-class family like his, without a doubt.

Lady Margaret's Grammar School occupied a collection of houses on the eastern side of Parsons Green. One, Belfield House, had been the home and studio of the artist Theodore Rousel, and the laboratory block was where the stables had been. Founded in 1917, the school's benefactors had included Sir Valentine Chirol, a former foreign editor of *The Times*, Dr Lyttleton, an ex-headmaster of Eton, and the wealthy Miss Carver. By the time I started in the first year in the autumn of 1958, the school was described as 'Church of England Voluntary Aided' and received a grant from the London County Council. Fees had been abolished and up to 400 girls were drawn from all over west London, with two forms making up each year.

Opposite St Dionis Church, the school had close links with the vicar, and regular services. The school motto was 'I have a goodly heritage' and girls were encouraged to seek out public service and charity work. The amount of homework was prodigious and soon I was studying French, Geography, History, Art, Algebra and English, with up to two hours of work each weekday evening. My new classmates came from a very wide background – their parents were everything from accountants to fine carpet dealers to policemen to civil servants. Some girls lived in large houses as far away as Hammersmith and Chiswick, others in council flats in the new Alton Estate in Roehampton by Wimbledon Common. One girl who lived there, Liz Mallison, soon became a close friend. Her mother was a social worker and a strong Labour supporter, and seemed far more approachable and sympathetic than my own mum. Liz was shorter than me, with dark short hair, cut in a bob, and soon we discovered that we liked the same kinds of clothes and music. Over the next couple of years I would spend more and more time at the weekends staying at Liz's flat, and we'd while away hours playing the same Buddy Holly records over and over again, something that simply wouldn't be tolerated at 18 Elmstone Road. Her home became a way to escape a lot of rules and curfews imposed by my parents.

*

I spent the first year at Lady Margaret's keeping my head down, anxious to fit in, very aware of how much more I now stood out as I walked down Parsons Green Lane to school sporting my new blazer and long cotton dress. At the end of the first term, my form mistress Miss Masaroon was pleased with my progress, and my report was littered with the wonderful word 'good' every line or so. On the last day of every term each girl was handed her report in a sealed brown envelope for her parents to read and sign. I would place it on the kitchen table and wait in trepidation for my father to open it. Throughout the first year I had no worries, because my reports were excellent and peace reigned at home, but I soon came to dread their reaction to reports of my undisciplined behaviour. My parents received a letter from Miss Marshall, the headmistress, saying that from the second year girls either studied Latin (necessary for entrance to many of the universities) or Biology (commonly thought to be the B division). Luckily I was selected for Latin, although I was never to show any aptitude for it whatsoever, but at least I was officially in the brainy class.

LADY MARGARET SCHOOL

REPORT   Name _Janet Bull._

Term _Autumn 1958_.   Form _IУ._   Average Age of Form _11¾._

Grades	Marks		
B.		SCRIPTURE	Good oral work, & usually good homework, but Janet must learn with care. _BEB_
		ENGLISH ...	Really good. Janet works well. _HEI_
B+		GEOGRAPHY ...	Janet works well and with enthusiasm. _E.H._
C		HISTORY ...	Janet shows enthusiasm in class but her written work is too often spoilt by carelessness. _E.H._
		LATIN ...	
C		FRENCH—WRITTEN	Janet must always give her full attention in class and do her written work carefully.
		ORAL	Her pronunciation is quite good. _CNK._
		ARITHMETIC ...	
B⁻		ALGEBRA ...	Janet's work is usually good, but she needs to
		GEOMETRY ...	work more accurately. _EP._
B+		SCIENCE ...	Good. Janet works with enthusiasm. _BWS._
B		ART	Good. _JVB._
B+		~~CRAFT~~ WRITING ...	Good. Janet's writing is clear and attractive. _W.W._
C+		MUSIC	Janet is working well. _D.S._
		INSTRUMENTAL MUSIC	Janet has made a very good start. _E.C._
B+		HOUSECRAFT ...	Good. Janet works very well. _EaT._
C		PHYSICAL EDUCATION	Good. Janet has worked well. _MEM_
		DANCING ...	

General Progress and Conduct:-

Janet is always enthusiastic and she must see that this pleasing trait is always allied to accurate work.

Times Absent ___

Time Late ___

Next Term _Jan 6._ to _March 25._

Half Term Holiday _Feb. 16 & 17._

Form Mistress _M.B. Jasaroon._

Head Mistress _EE Marshall_

Parent's Signature _RG Bull._

I had a busy time in my first two years, with plenty of extra-curricular activities to keep me out of trouble and away from the gaze of my parents. One activity I really enjoyed was playing the piano, and I had a lesson a week after school. I practised on an old upright which my parents bought and placed in the front sitting room we never used, and took my examinations once a year at the Royal College of Music in South Kensington. I also went to life-saving classes at Fulham Baths, which was ludicrous really, because I was so short-sighted that if anyone was drowning at sea I certainly couldn't have seen them without my thick specs on. In October 1959 I went to my first classical concerts with Auntie Eileen, the Robert Mayer Proms for young people at the Royal Festival Hall on Saturday mornings. Joan Sutherland sang the Mad Scene from Donizetti's *Lucia di Lammermoor*, and I was totally hooked by the emotional rollercoaster of the piece. I also belonged to the art club at the Natural History Museum and would travel up to South Kensington by myself on Saturday mornings and spend hours sketching on a large sheet of white paper pinned to a wooden board – everything from dinosaurs to eagles. I even went through a brief phase of athletics with my friend Vicky Wise, who lived in the next road to us. We would spend one night a week running in Hurlingham Park with the Spartan Ladies athletic club, and jogging around the streets doing distance training. Quite soon Vicky developed a real aptitude for the hurdles, but I had no real stamina and after a couple of months trying to achieve success with the long jump, I gave it up. I couldn't bear to be doing something if I wasn't the best!

By now, my natural rebelliousness was already beginning to show and my reports began to record my long-running battles with any figure of authority. Miss Hudd, my second-year form mistress, wrote, 'Janet must guard against being over-boisterous', and when I submitted an English essay entitled 'Escape from School' it was not well received. I began to work out it was best to deliver what they wanted to read, and in one essay, 'What I'd take on a desert island', I opted for a hammer and nails, a piano, a book about plants and the Bible. Unimpressed, the teacher wrote 'DO NOT EVER USE A BALL POINT PEN AGAIN' across the bottom. My helter-skelter approach to subjects I wasn't that interested in was especially evident when it came to Geography – I scored A one term and D the next. I adored English Literature, Drama and Poetry, and would spend hours in the top floor art studios painting and drawing after classes had ended. One of my favourite subjects, Housecraft, abruptly came to an end after two years. During all the time I had spent applying myself to this weird 'craft', I still had not progressed beyond things that started with the letter A. I could make an apron, an apple crumble, baked apple and apple fool, but never made it as far as an artichoke or asparagus before Spanish replaced cooking in my curriculum.

Meanwhile, my reports mixed the good news with the bad: 'Janet must not relax her efforts to maintain self-control' got me into real trouble at home, written after a childish stunt when I had stacked up lines and lines of empty bottles outside the staffroom while the teachers were having a meeting. I hid out of sight after ringing the fire alarm bell and collapsed in hysterics when several of the most pompous teachers dashed out of the door and fell over my bottles and on to the floor. The row that precipitated was nothing compared to the one after the end-of-year report which stated 'Janet's ability to do well is offset by her lack of concentration'. I remember not producing it until Saturday morning, propping it up against the milk jug on the kitchen table and dreading the moment when my father would tear open the envelope over breakfast. Hours of recriminations followed with the endless mantras about 'wasting my opportunities', 'why did I spend so much time showing off' and finally the inevitable 'If you don't behave you won't be allowed to go out, and MARK MY WORDS MY GIRL I'LL TEACH YOU A LESSON YOU BLOODY WELL WON'T FORGET.'

By 1961 I'd passed my Grade Three piano exam, and got a silver medal in the Rounders Tournament. I had started hanging out in the record shop on the other side of Parsons Green, listening to Duke Ellington and Dave Brubeck after classes had ended with Liz, getting chatted up by the bloke behind the counter. Now my reports read 'Janet's behaviour shows a lack of consideration for others' after I had been caught staging another prank, this time locking people in the changing room after hockey.

'Janet must be less talkative' was another rage-inducing remark in my end-of-year report. It was odd that I was so terrified of failing to live up to the educational standards demanded by my parents, two people whose formal education had ended at fourteen. Every time I got into trouble at school, both of them would start a long-winded whine about all the sacrifices they were making for me, how I was throwing away opportunities they never had (both of which were undoubtedly true as my uniform and piano lessons must have cost quite a bit). My mother never failed to tell me just how exactly like her I was, although I never quite understood what she meant — in retrospect perhaps she meant quick and intelligent, as she had been at my age — and my father never stopped threatening to take me away from school unless I tried harder to behave. 'AND YOU CAN TAKE THAT BLOODY LOOK OFF YOUR FACE WHILE I'M TALKING TO YOU OTHERWISE I'LL BLOODY KNOCK IT OFF AND THEN YOU'LL REALLY HAVE SOMETHING TO LOOK SULKY ABOUT.' Meanwhile it was suggested by one of my teachers that my career prospects might be better in the long term if I had elocution lessons, but luckily my parents wouldn't hear of it.

*

I'd started keeping a diary, noting down exactly what I saw on television, what books I read and what clothes I was making – I was plotting my escape from the stifling world at home through ruthless self-improvement. My best friends at school were Liz and Ed (real name Christine) from my class at school. Over the next year or so Liz and I would evolve into mods, going to see live music in St Mary's Ballroom off Putney High Street or at clubs like the Scene in the West End. We were fanatically picky about what we'd wear, and ruthless when it came to boys. If they lived south of the river in naff places like Wandsworth or Clapham we simply didn't bother talking to them any more. After one boy I'd met at the youth club took me to the cinema in Fulham Broadway and I came home sporting his ring, my mother went ballistic: 'NO DAUGHTER OF MINE IS GETTING ENGAGED TO A BRITISH RAIL WAITER – GET THAT BLOODY RING OFF YOUR FINGER AT ONCE.' I pulled it off and never wore it again. It wasn't even an engagement ring, but the reaction it provoked was intense. She felt that I was being educated at great expense and there was no way I was going to end up with someone of a lower social order, in her eyes. To be honest, I agreed with her, I hadn't really thought through what wearing someone's ring might mean to them. Years later it emerged that she'd been engaged three times, but of course my mother never considered herself a hypocrite. But now at 18 Elmstone Road my parents and I were officially at war and things weren't going to get any more agreeable.

6

Suburbia

'I only wanted something else to do but hang around.'
Pet Shop Boys' lyric to 'Suburbia'

IT WAS A COLD January evening and the Christmas decorations had been taken down at Elmstone Road, the wrapping paper folded up to be reused, and the best cards cut up into labels to use on presents next year. The festive season was well and truly over, and the new term had started at school. The fire was burning in the grate and we were sitting in the kitchen one Monday night eating tea of stew made with corned beef, carrots and potatoes at 6 o'clock. Then they dropped the bombshell.

'We're moving,' my father casually announced to my sister and me as Mum put the food in front of us. 'To Perivale.'

He might as well have said Afghanistan or Mars, I had no idea where they were talking about. The western extremities of the Central Line were quite outside my experience. We had no relatives or close friends there at all. They told us that our house in Fulham had been sold, for £5,000, to a Greek hairdresser and his family who were to move in within a month. My sister had been taken in the car a few weeks earlier to look at some new housing estates being built in Barnet, near my grandmother's house in Southgate. I wasn't on that particular outing and hadn't realised what was going on as both parents spoke in code in front of us when it involved anything major.

My father had wanted to buy a house near his parents, but it turned out that none of the properties would be ready by the time the hairdresser was to move in. The crisis was resolved when Cyril, a workmate of my dad's, told him about an empty house near his on the outskirts of Ealing. Having viewed it the previous weekend with Mum, my father had snapped it up, without showing it to either my sister or me. Mum would have been pleased — as he had already decided we needed to move and wouldn't be budged, at least she wouldn't have the dreaded Nana Bull living around the corner. Now, as usual, he'd just issued the children with the minimum information necessary. That was his style: no chit-chat, no discussion. We were never offered any explanation for the move, it was presented as a fait accompli. Conversations on such matters did not take place in our household — our thoughts and opinions were of no consequence whatsoever. One reason for the move might have been his father's recent death, and the fact my nana was ill in hospital, and proving to be a very difficult and demanding patient. Who knows? In fact he was making the worst economic decision of his life, moving from Fulham less than ten years before it became a highly sought-after overspill area for the middle classes who wanted to be near Chelsea. Our house would have been worth hundreds of thousands of pounds if we'd stayed put.

To this day I cannot believe how cruel this decision was, to uproot me at fourteen from the place where I not only attended school, worked in the library at the end of our street, had been to Brownies and the Girl Guides, belonged to the running club and, most importantly, attended the youth club next to St Dionis Church on Parsons Green. Fulham was the epicentre of my entire world. I knew all the streets, the shops, the parks, the local gangs. We played rounders on Parsons Green, tennis in Hurlingham Park, walked across Eel Brook Common to Fulham Broadway and through South Park to the River Thames. I'd learned to swim in Fulham Baths and had the only dolly I'd ever owned mended at the Dolls' Hospital

off Fulham Broadway. Of course my mother hadn't come from Fulham in the first place — it was where my father had been born and brought up, even though his parents had long moved away. But, even so, plunged into commuting right across London for hours on end, denied the possibility of hanging around the neighbourhood after school, going to local events and just doing what every other teenager at my school was doing – staring at boys outside the record shop, going to cafes, buying a Wimpy. Before the new school term had started in January, I'd been round to Juana Knapp's house and spent hours in her bedroom listening to records, then a few days later we'd gone next door to Vicky Wise's house and done the same thing. I'd travelled on the Underground up to the High Street Kensington branch of C & A after school and bought a skirt in the sale. I even went to the Guides meeting wearing black stockings – the ultimate in teenage protest. At the optician's in Fulham Broadway I'd bought some new glasses, and got drunk at my friend's party in Putney one Friday night while my parents were out, swigging Ye Olde Shakespeare cooking sherry at two shillings and sixpence a bottle and getting up on Saturday just to sleep off my hangover in Bishop's Park while the crowds streamed past en route to football at Craven Cottage. All normal adolescent behaviour. This cosy existence I knew so well was suddenly terminated forever. But why Perivale, of all places?

My father had rented an allotment in this part of Ealing for a year or so, after he gave up on the one he'd had in Bishop's Park near Fulham Football Ground. The new allotment was near the river, and frequently flooded, but he didn't seem to mind, enjoying the drive to and from it as an escape from the domestic dramas in Fulham. His workmate Cyril lived nearby on a dreary housing estate just off the A40 after Hanger Lane; there was only one road in and out of this forgettable series of cul-de-sacs which just about summed it up. You entered from the thundering traffic on the four-lane dual carriageway via a parade of completely uninspiring local shops, a newsagent, chemist, butcher and greengrocer. There was a chip shop — I would soon be a regular, lurking around outside it several nights a week — and a church, built at the same time as the estate, with a hall next to it, where the youth club was held every Wednesday and Friday. Every bloody street looked exactly the same, with pairs of semi-detached villas in two styles, one with mock Tudor gables, the other with stucco façades and rounded 1930s bay windows.

The only building of any note locally was the wonderful Hoover Factory on the other side of the playing fields by our road, an Art Deco temple of high style, modelled on the Parthenon. I would occasionally go to dances in the workers' club at the rear, discovering that the interior of the building in no way matched up to the breathtaking façade with its glittering chevrons of red, blue and green ceramic tiling, and its gorgeous green-painted geometric iron gates.

Now my mother was thrilled that at 2 Bleasdale Avenue we had our own front door, and my sister and I had a bedroom each. I, of course, managed to get the biggest one, at the back of the house, but as it had the linen cupboard and water heater in one corner there was no sense of privacy as my mother was constantly in and out of it on the pretext of getting a clean tea towel or turning the immersion heater on. Being on the corner of the road, I felt curiously exposed, unused to so much space around one side of our house after the narrow gardens of Fulham. Here we had a wrought-iron gate and a paved area at the front of the house in which were planted roses. At the side was a ramshackle garage, but Dad soon knocked it down to make a paved area for the family car. At the rear was a small garden, and at the bottom of it an old air-raid shelter covered in pebbledash concrete. My father immediately dug up half of the back garden and turned it into another allotment, planting onions, runner beans and carrots where once had been dahlias, daisies and a herbaceous border. Our lawn, the pleasure area for sunbathing and lolling about, was radically diminished by his determination that we should be as self-sufficient as possible (as his parents had been during the war). He commandeered the air-raid shelter and soon it was a no-go area for all us womenfolk, as he filled it with ancient televisions he intended to repair at some future date, and dusty cabinets full of all the paraphernalia of a compulsive DIY addict: screws, saws, aerials, tins of paint, hammers, string, plugs and wire.

Inside our new home the bathroom was tiny, the toilet on the upstairs landing little more than a cupboard with zero privacy. Ugly night-storage heaters my father had nicked from jobs he was doing for the council stood like grey metal tombstones in every room, chucking out heat at exactly the time you didn't want it: when you were asleep. At least in Elmstone Road we had higher ceilings, Victorian tiles in our hall, plaster mouldings on the ceiling in the front room, stained glass in the front door.

Here the back room contained a new dining table and four chairs, and a sideboard full of cutlery and plates. The front room had a television, sofa and a couple of Ercol armchairs upholstered in floral-patterned tapestry in tasteful autumnal shades. The kitchen was a galley, no more. The whole place felt claustrophobic from the outset.

I was allowed to choose the wallpaper for my bedroom, and selected a lurid scene of bullfighters in orange and black on a white background. It was thought to be very expensive, so I was only allowed it in one alcove – the rest of the room was in standard-issue, good taste, beige and green stripes. My sister's bedroom was so small it contained a single bed, a chest of drawers and nothing else.

This sense of living in each other's pockets wasn't just confined to the home. Now my father was to drive to work in London each day – he was an electrical engineer for Middlesex County Council based in Westminster, and my mother had a job as a clerical assistant in Holland Park Tax Office based in Holland Park Avenue, near Shepherd's Bush. In order to save money it was decided that we would all commute to work by car each day, one week in my father's car and the next week in Cyril's Mini. At 7.45 a.m. precisely my mother and I would be crammed into the back of a small car, the two men sitting in the front (and smoking), and we entered the rush-hour hell of the A40. We would drop my mother off outside her office in west London, then I would be deposited near

Earl's Court tube station, from which I would get the District Line to Parsons Green. My dad and his mate would finish the drive to their office in time for a 9 a.m. start.

I cannot describe the horribleness of sitting squashed up like a praying mantis in the back of a small car full of smoke and men talking interminably about football or traffic jams. I could hardly extend my arms enough to read my school textbooks or finish my homework. I was expected to be seen and not heard. The windows were completely opaque as the car steamed up with the heat emanating from four six-foot-tall people all clad in winter overcoats. Ugh! The joy of the odd morning when I was allowed to walk to the station and travel for twenty minutes into Notting Hill Gate, and then wait for a Wimbledon train via Earl's Court! One day a man had a heart attack and died right by me on the train between Perivale and Park Royal. I thought it was an omen.

At least the journey home would be made alone each day, in my own time, but as it always took at least an hour I could no longer just hang around Fulham with my friends. We had moved in the middle of my exams and, not surprisingly, my report at the end of that term was not very good. 'Lack of attention . . . insufficient effort . . . needs more discipline' were all familiar phrases, but no one ever took me on one side at school and asked me how on earth I was coping with the journey from hell — I was surely travelling further than anyone in my class, but perhaps no one thought that mattered. A lot of homework got done between Notting Hill Gate and Perivale, and if I got really bogged down in it I'd often look up and find I'd passed my stop and was in West Ruislip, still struggling with some awful French or Spanish translation. In the exercise books, my handwriting would be sloping in the direction the tube was travelling. Or I'd sit on the train silently mouthing the set books I tried to learn by heart for Latin, reciting passages from the *Aeneid* Book 8 over and over again as we left Shepherd's Bush and the dark tunnels of central London behind and emerged into the daylight and the factories and car scrap yards of East Acton.

It was no easier for my sister — she'd been uprooted from her single-sex grammar school in Fulham after just one and a bit terms and dropped into Elliott Green, a mixed one in Ealing, with new classmates as well as new neighbours, in an unfamiliar place on a new route to school. The headmaster turned out to be a friend of our father's – so my sister also felt under surveillance in her own particular way. Her classwork immediately suffered and she made very little effort to pass any exams whatsoever over the coming years.

My parents became very close to Cyril and his wife, who lived further down our street, but for years we were still to commute to Fulham to see Auntie Vi at weekends, and on Wednesdays my father would always drive over to Southgate to see his mother, often taking all of us with him. Looking back on it, an incredible amount of time was spent just driving, trying to keep all the strands of family life together. My father continued to support his football team, Fulham, at home games every other Saturday, dropping my mother off at her sister's house first and returning there for tea at 5.30 or 6 o'clock afterwards.

I had hardly any time to make new friends in Perivale before it was Easter and we all got in the bloody car again and drove for six hours up the A5 to spend the next two weeks staying with my nain in Llanfairfechan. Once in

North Wales I would hang out with some of the local girls, visit the small amusements arcade on the beach, and watch films in the local fleapit. Llanfairfechan felt even more claustrophobic than Perivale – my sister and I still shared a bed and spent each night kicking each other and squabbling as its ancient mattress sagged so badly we were forever rolling down into the middle of the bed. My mother would storm upstairs and place a long bolster between us, dividing the bed into two separate zones.

I cried one night because I knew that Liz, my school friend, and her parents were having a party at their flat in Putney and I was stuck in bloody North Wales in a small stone cottage with nothing to do, no television, rainy weather and just my parents and Pat for company. After the holidays I went back to school and the grim commuting started again. My sister went for a weekend away with friends in a caravan. I wrote in my diary: 'I am so lonely, I wish I was anywhere else . . .' By now I wanted to go and see jazz concerts with Thelonius Monk or the Modern Jazz Quartet at Hammersmith or Victoria, but living in Perivale made it very difficult. I started to go to the local youth club and gradually made a couple of friends nearby, but these were very different from the girls I knew at grammar school – these girls' aspirations lay in becoming mums or hairdressers, whereas we Lady Margaret young ladies were always being told that further education at college or university was our goal. Boys in Perivale were trainee builders or plumbers. It was a fairly ordinary group of working-class teenagers I began to mix with, but they were better than having no friends at all.

Over the next few years I would still spend hours on the train every week going to clubs and parties in Fulham and Putney with my classmates Liz and Ed. I played rounders, tennis and netball in the school teams and we often had away matches after school, meaning I spent even more time getting to and from suburbia. For some reason my mother started attending church in Perivale. I couldn't imagine why, as she had shown little interest in it in Fulham – perhaps she too was lonely and it was a way of meeting other women her age. She tried to make me go to Sunday morning service with her but I told her to forget it and there was a screaming row. Attending a church school, I had enough religion shoved down my throat all week, thanks a lot.

Always style-conscious, I now spent hours making my own clothes, and then had an 'urchin' cut down at the shops in Perivale and immediately hated it. Even the hairdressers near my new home were useless. I would go up to town on most Saturdays, staying with Auntie Vi in Fulham or my friend Liz in Roehampton. My mother immediately started picking fights, saying I went out too often. A pattern was emerging which would continue until I finally baled out. I now had all the times of the last trains home written in my diary.

The only other source of entertainment in Perivale

was dances at the local sports clubs and factories and the British Legion – hardly very exciting, as they generally included the adults. By the summer I had one firm 'local' friend, Joanie, who lived just down the road from the church.

A year older than me, she was good fun and always up for a night of playing records or jiving at the youth club. There, the local boys would make fun of my hair and glasses, and I didn't fit too well into the conformist mentality of those born into a semi-detached world. I felt torn between two sets of friends, not old enough to go in pubs or on holiday by myself. I was still trapped in a whole lot of family rituals, like the interminable car drive around the North Circular to Southgate each Wednesday evening to have supper with my nana, who had definitely taken a turn for the worse since my granddad had died. She had returned home from hospital and was living alone. Always eccentric, she now barely spoke, and certainly not to my mother who she seemed to ignore.

Nana also lived in a semi-d, but it was older and larger than ours, with antique furniture. After tea, the evening would seem very long and boring, punctuated by the loud ticking of the clock on her mantelpiece. As my father chatted sporadically to his mother and my mother did the washing-up, I would read old copies of *Reader's Digest* from the bookcase. When the clock chimed nine we all got in the car and drove back to Perivale, duty done for another week. There would be frequent arguments in the car on the way home, and my parents would often arrive back to Bleasdale Avenue in stony silence.

But they were still thrilled to be living in Perivale, no matter what I or my sister felt. To them suburbia represented everything modern and practical. When my cousin visited from Wales we all got in the car and took her to London Airport, to see the planes taking off – how exciting! Then it was on the Underground and up to visit the shops on Oxford Street, with tea at Lyons' Corner House at Marble Arch. Gradually I got used to the commuting, even getting a job at Woolworths in Shepherd's Bush after school. To my astonishment I was asked to take an intelligence test to make sure I was smart enough to be a shop assistant, hilarious really, as I was studying for eight O-levels, including pure and applied mathematics. The test seemed to involve adding up the cost of a lot of light bulbs and pairs of woollen socks and subtracting them from a ten pound note. Luckily I passed with flying colours and was issued with a pale-green nylon overall, which had a very fitted bodice and a long, unflattering circular skirt. I looked demented in it, standing by the till behind the sock counter.

although I felt no affection for the place whatsoever. After we had lived there for just over two years I came home from school one June afternoon to find the house empty. My sister's school was a short journey away by train and she usually arrived home before me – I thought that maybe she had stayed behind in detention or gone to a cafe in Greenford with her friends. I was revising for my O-levels, which were starting the following week, and so I shut the door of my bedroom and got on with trying to master Virgil's *Aeneid* Book 8 for the umpteenth time. My mother came home from work in the tax office, walking from the station, and then at around 6.30 my father drove up in the car. No sign of my sister. By now, they were worried and started telephoning her friends. No one had seen her. By 9 p.m. they were frantic, and my mother started screaming at me about Pat – surely I knew what she was up to? Of course my sister and I hardly communicated. I knew none of her friends, and I certainly didn't have a clue where she was. To me she was an alien being who simply lived in the horrid little front bedroom, and all conversation between us was kept to a minimum. As she went to school locally she had severed ties with Fulham whereas I had not, and I had no idea how she spent her time or who she hung out with in Perivale.

My parents drove down to the nearest police station and returned looking grim at 10.30. My mother sat up, waiting for the phone to ring. She called her sister and there was a lot of jabbering in Welsh. I went to bed and pulled the pillow over my head, trying to shut the developing drama out of my mind.

Next morning I went to school on the train and both of my parents drove to Pat's school and discovered she hadn't been there the previous day. When I returned home later they both looked completely shattered. I was sure that Pat had just buggered off for a bit of a break. Like me, she was probably sick of the tense atmosphere at home and the constant bickering between our parents. I wasn't that worried, but my mother most definitely was fearing the worst, and kept dissolving into floods of tears. A police car drew up outside and the two men inside were shown into our front room, where my father shut the door firmly so I should not hear anything. Later I found they were compiling a description of my sister and trying to work out what she might have been wearing.

Sitting in my bedroom, revising and bored to tears, I noticed that the top drawer in my dressing table had been opened. My post office book was missing. I used it to deposit my earnings from babysitting and Woolworths, saving up for clothes and records. We were given a pound a week each pocket money, but we had to do at least three hours' housework every Sunday in order to earn it. I had been allotted the ironing for about six months now, a task I completely loathed. My pocket money never made it into the post office book, as it got spent on admission to local clubs and dances. My savings were for more special treats for myself, and so I was quite miffed that the cheeky cow had made off with it. But at the same time, I was secretly jealous – what style, what cunning, what resourcefulness. Her bid for freedom was totally impressive!

After four days, I was told that my sister's description was going to be released to the press and would be on the evening news next day. Now I really was sick with envy. My sister was going to be famous. Somehow I knew no harm had come to her, in spite of my mother's endless snivelling. Late that night a phone call from the police told my parents that a young girl answering my sister's description had been spotted in Bangor, North Wales, and they were going to a boarding house to pick her up. Within twenty-four hours she was home, cowed but not showing the slightest sign of remorse. She'd cashed £15 from my savings, checked herself into a bed and breakfast saying she was visiting relatives, and spent the time wandering around Bangor and Menai, eating in cafes and hanging out in amusement arcades. On her arrival home, she was ordered to bed, and the police and my parents closeted themselves in the front room again. Later, after they had gone, my mother came to my room and said that the detectives had thought it best not to question my sister about her motives, and everyone thought it would be a good idea not to mention the events of the last four days, in case she did it again.

And so, incredibly, life continued at 2 Bleasdale Avenue as if nothing had happened. No mention was ever made of my fourteen-year-old sister's extraordinary journey, to Euston station and on to North Wales. My father paid the missing money back into my post office book and we just carried on with our daily routines: I completed my O-levels, my sister went back to school and life in suburbia just ground on as before. Twenty-five years later when my mother died I finally asked my sister why she'd made her bid for freedom. Just for a laugh, she said – 'I was bored to tears in Perivale, and I just fancied a holiday.' I had been right all along. Before she died my mother had given Pat an even more bizarre piece of information. It seemed that when my sister was brought back home and sent to bed, the policemen who talked to our parents in our front room had recommended the family embarked on some form of counselling – it was felt it would be a good idea if we sat together and tried to discuss what my sister had done, to prevent her doing it again, and to try and make her feel more at ease within the family. But of course we did the complete opposite. My mother never apologised or explained her actions, and my father died decades later without ever mentioning Pat's great escape from suburbia again. As usual it was airbrushed from our lives.

7

Je Suis une Mod

WE SAT IN ARMCHAIRS either side of the hissing gas fire, me carefully balancing a plate of cheese and a large hunk of baguette on my knees, with a glass of red wine at my feet. Edith Piaf was warbling 'Non! Rien de rien . . . Non! Je ne regrette rien', out of the wind-up gramophone on the sideboard for the tenth time in an hour. Another Saturday afternoon in Notting Hill Gate with my eccentric godmother Eileen. During the Piaf serenade I had struggled to converse in halting French, reading slowly from a copy of *Paris Match* purchased down the road in Queensway. We were lunching off provisions from the impressive food hall at Whiteleys department store, a vast hall with wide aisles stacked full of exotic

salamis and cheeses, marrons glacés and stuffed olives –
exotica that never graced our table in suburban Perivale.
After lunch Eileen and I were all set to take a leisurely

stroll down to the Coronet cinema at the Gate to see the afternoon screening of *La Testament d'Orphée* for the second time in a month.

My auntie Eileen might have fallen out with my mother over her fling with my dad, but after she re-established herself at the centre of our small family group, she took the business of being my godmother very seriously, and decided to educate me in her own bizarre way. Most Saturday mornings from the age of ten, I would be put on the number 28 bus in Fulham Road, getting off around the corner from her flat in Westbourne Grove, at the northern end of Notting Hill Gate. As I grew older and we moved to Perivale, the visits decreased in frequency, but Eileen exercised a tremendous influence on my cultural life for at least five years, deciding what films I saw and suggesting books to read. She took me to plays in French, Italian neo-realist movies like *La Strada* and *The Rose Tattoo*, and paid for regular trips to the ballet and opera at Covent Garden and Sadler's Wells, treating me as a younger companion rather than a child.

By the time I was eighteen, I was a fully formed cultural elitist, and had soaked up more art cinema and been exposed to more of the operatic repertoire than anyone else in my year at college. As for my parents, they were relieved that someone else was happy to spend time with their increasingly sulky and stroppy elder daughter. Around Eileen I was none of those things – for a start she was introducing me to a new world with endless fresh and exhilarating possibilities. My horizons were broadening beyond Fulham Broadway and the ABC Regal cinema, the record shop and Barbers' haberdashery department.

It was very difficult to separate fact from fiction with my auntie Eileen – my mother told me Eileen had been engaged to a man who had jilted her, leaving her heartbroken. She was also supposed to have been a junior member of the ballet at Covent Garden in her youth, and certainly knew a lot of the staff when she took me to matinees. Winnie, the jolly barmaid, would hoist me up on to the counter and pour me glasses of orange squash, making sure there were cushions for me to sit on in my seat at the back of the stalls, so I was raised up enough to get a good view.

Eileen certainly cultivated an air of mystery which was appealing to a gawky ten-year-old. She refused to wear black, claiming it was 'ageing' and always wore an immaculate series of navy blue suits, coats and sweaters, with white silk blouses and tasteful jewellery, her hair in a chignon. She was small-boned and graceful, so she probably had learnt ballet, but by the time I was growing up she had left her wartime job with the Civil Service and was a bookkeeper working in a series of offices in west London. I later found out that she had never been engaged to anyone, but had been completely infatuated with a man called Richard Austin, a conductor with the Bournemouth Philharmonic Orchestra who was married with children. She still kept framed photographs of him on the sideboard in her flat. It seems he had never reciprocated her feelings in any way, and she'd only ever met him by hanging around the stage door after concerts and queuing for his autograph when she and my mother first came to live in London after the war had ended.

When kicked out of our part of 18 Elmstone Road by my mother, Eileen had taken a room in a large house on Westbourne Grove, owned by two Estonian refugees, Mr and Mrs Kask. Over the next twenty years they would be extremely kind to her, treating her as one of their own were divided into a warren of bedsits and small flats run by people like the notorious slum landlord Peter Rachmann, and rented out to a transient population of West Indians, Irish, Poles, French people, Latvians and Estonians. Queensway was a cosmopolitan meeting place with foreign newspapers and magazines on sale in the tobacconists', and inviting patisseries where you could linger over a delicious croissant or rum baba. Whiteleys department store, occupying a whole block, was the focal point, with its cool tiled black and white mosaic floors, a breathtaking, curving Art Nouveau staircase at its centre, and impressive towers at the corners of the building. Far grander than Barbers in Fulham, it had departments selling everything from furniture to electrical goods, fabrics and makeup.

I started learning French formally at grammar school when I was eleven, but Eileen used to insist we spoke it for a couple of hours on Saturdays. She was obsessed with all things français, from chanson, to food, to the cinema. Another anthem she would play over and over again was Charles Trenet moodily singing 'La Mer', recorded in 1946, just after the war had ended. His wonderful voice, smoky and full of pathos, would almost make me cry every time I heard it. We went to see the distinguished actress Edwige Feullière performing in French, part of an international theatre season in the West End. Of course I only understood one word in ten, but the experience was unforgettable – the soft rise and fall of her musical voice as she stood in the middle of a deserted stage, playing a passenger on a boat travelling through the tropics.

Eileen was introducing me to a world, via the theatre and cinema, which was magical and challenging. We went to the Royal Festival Hall where I sat spellbound listening to the Austrian soprano Elisabeth Schwarzkopf singing lieder and I must have seen Jean Cocteau's surrealist fairy story *La Belle et La Bête* at least three times before I was twelve. I had memorised every scene and would draw versions of Jean Marais's amazing cat-like makeup in my sketchbooks. I dreamt of the hall where Beauty walks through a long line of white curtains, where the wall lights are candles held by bare arms. I lapped up all these experiences eagerly, keeping notes and sketchbooks, lists and diaries, pictures cut from magazines. Of course Eileen was lonely, without much of a family, no boyfriend, and a

read during the year, from *The New Poetry* edited by Al
Alvarez to *Restless Heart* by Jean Anouilh. Eileen's influence
was still strong, and I struggled through *Ripening Seed* by
Colette in French, to please her. I was reading a lot of
poetry, and going to see Christopher Logue recite his verse
accompanied by a jazz band at a pub in west London, the
very latest craze. He'd stand on a stage in a smoky room
reeling off verses about love, lust and the nuclear bomb at
a frantic pace. Even though I thought it was pretty exciting,
the last thing I would do in public was show any emotion.
Mods didn't do that, it was all part of our 'cool' impene-
trable façade. Being a mod wasn't just about clothes and
music, but attitude as well. I read a lot of drama, from
John Osborne's *Luther* to Arthur Miller's *Death of a Salesman*
and *Baby Doll* by Tennessee Williams. In short, I was an
uneasy mixture of sophistication and naivety, unable to
converse easily and gauche and unsure of myself with men.
My tastes were certainly eclectic – I would go to St Mary's
Ballroom in Putney regularly on Saturday nights with Liz
to see Johnny Kidd and the Pirates, or Vince Eager and
Shane Fenton with all the other Fulham and Putney mods,
and then spend hours drinking a cup of coffee in the

and follow them home on the Underground from Leicester Square tube station – they were sharing a large flat off the Fulham Road, on the borders of Chelsea and Fulham. They were simply fantastic. It wasn't possible to be in that crowded basement in Soho listening to 'Little Red Rooster' and not be knocked out. Loud, rough, raunchy and hot, they were my absolute favourites, but all these club nights were packed out after they made their first television appearance on *Thank Your Lucky Stars* in June.

By the summer of 1963, Eileen had decided to leave London and had taken a job as a bookkeeper in Jersey, renting a flat in a large house in the countryside outside St Helier. I promised that I'd go out and stay with her during my summer holiday. I read about ten pages of a book on Zen Buddhism and realised that I was more interested in dyeing my hair with the new wonder lightener Poly Blonde than following any new route to spiritual enlightenment. I would spend hours doctoring patterns on our dining table, copying dresses from *Queen* magazine or *Vogue* in fabrics I'd buy at Pontings department store in Kensington High Street. I would pay regular visits to a hairdresser there, having abandoned the local one in Perivale. I had my hair cut in a severe mod bob. I bought a leather jacket but couldn't wear it until it had been 'aged' by getting screwed up under my mattress for a fortnight.

In June, while the Profumo scandal erupted in Parliament and the national press, I was more concerned about getting myself on camera when Liz and I appeared in the audience of *Easy Beat* at the ATV studios in Wembley, dancing like true mods with blank facial expressions, shoulders held stiffly like coathangers, and our elbows stuck out at angles. I found my first television appearance an exciting experience and later in the year I managed to get into the audience on the new pop show *Ready Steady Go*, also recorded at Wembley and presented by Queen of the Mods Kathy McGowan.

O-Levels out of the way, Liz and I were allowed to go on holiday by ourselves for the first time in August, because we were staying with my godmother Eileen and it was assumed that we would be reasonably well behaved. The first thing we did on arrival was to go and queue for tickets for the Beatles at the Springfield Ballroom. We spent the next few days pretending to be interested in the sights, doing a minimal amount of sunbathing at St

Brelade's Bay, and a considerable amount of time hanging out in pubs and trying to catch the eye of any bloke aged about eighteen and single — there weren't very many. I stuck a new ash-blonde rinse on my hair — perhaps that would do the trick — and we went to the Springfield Ballroom twice in our first week, but didn't manage to score more than a drink off a couple of friendly mod boys from Richmond. The annual carnival, the Battle of Flowers — a parade of floats decked out with roses and daisies and festooned with local beauties in bathing suits — seemed a dud tourist event to me, even more unimpressive as it poured with rain.

Then, on the afternoon of Tuesday August the 6th, Liz and I were moodily mincing along a road on the outskirts of St Helier when we saw a smart open-topped sports car approaching with four long-haired boys in it. Immediately I totally lost my cool. 'LIZ LIZ LIZ . . . IT'S THE BEATLES . . . HI . . . HI . . . HI . . .' I screamed my head off as they slowly cruised past, spotted us, turned and waved. For five seconds I had forgotten every single thing I'd taught myself about being cool, every mod mantra I'd adopted for the last two years vanished out of the window. I gathered up my long narrow pencil slim skirt and chased them down the street babbling hysterically, 'HI HI HI . . .' but they'd gone, leaving a street full of middle-aged couples shopping in their hideous holiday shorts looking at me as if I was having an epileptic fit. That night, when we returned from the pub, I could hardly sleep with excitement. Would they spot us from the stage of the

Springfield? Would they wave again? I was besotted. I had seen them play once in a club in London, but that was when they were just starting out, still too rock and roll for my taste. Now it was different: the Beatles had started their UK tour in February and the BBC had presented a whole radio series about them. They were hot!

We got to the Springfield Ballroom early, but being mods meant that we had decided to stand at the back, where we could dance and show off our cool moves. Slobbering and crying down at the front and shaking our heads in time to the music with the other besotted females just wasn't our style. Nevertheless I was ecstatic – the band was just so full of energy and so exciting, I could hardly breathe. I never wanted them to stop playing. What a great way to end our holiday!

Next day we flew home and I returned to a holiday job my mother had got me working as a temporary clerical assistant in the Holland Park Tax Office. I spent most of my time opening the post and sending out form P92s, apart from one disastrous spell when I was assigned temporary switchboard duty and managed to cut most people off. Like driving, it was not a skill I was ready to

21 OCT 1964
SIX BELLS JAZZ CLUB

SIX BELLS, KING'S ROAD,

CHELSEA.

MEMBERSHIP CARD

- 2 OCT 1964

MEMBERS NAME ....

KLOOKS KLEEK

no. 12517

jazz at the

RAILWAY HOTEL
west hampstead

SIGNATURE:

STUDIO 51
10-11 GREAT NEWPORT ST.
LEICESTER SQ.

RHYTHM & BLUES

★ *every Friday 8.00 pm.*
★ *every Sunday afternoon 4-6.30.*
★ *every Monday 8.00 pm.*

Bring this card with you

master. When the autumn term started I was in the sixth form, which meant more relaxed rules about school uniform. Thank God I no longer had to wear a gymslip or navy skirt – I made a plain tweed, narrow mod skirt and bought a couple of sweaters, one daringly crocheted. I planned to retake Latin (which I had just failed for the second time) and started work on four A-levels: art, history, English and mathematics – I was keeping all my options open as I had no career plans whatsoever, much to my parents' annoyance. I also worked out that the more I studied, the more time I would have by myself for 'revision'. In fact, I would smuggle *Melody Maker* into the school library and spend most of my days plotting my night life, which revolved around my new favourite club, the Six Bells in Chelsea, where Alexis Korner hosted a blues night on Thursdays.

Over the past year I hadn't got very far with boys at all. Being a cool miserable-looking mod was one thing, but to actually get a bloke to penetrate that formidable façade and ask you for a dance or buy you a drink was a problem. I'd been on a handful of dates, but no one, it seemed, ever wanted to take me out more than once. Instead of trying to impress the local boys in Perivale, I gradually accepted that they were a pretty uninteresting bunch. I developed a thick skin, used to being rejected. They might think I looked funny with my mod clothes and glasses, but I thought I looked pretty hip. I spent a lot of evenings down at the Ealing Jazz Club, where a new band, Manfred Mann, really impressed me.

By now I had sent off for the membership forms and paid my subs to sign up to the CND movement, inspired by the huge number of people who had marched from Aldermaston to London earlier in the spring. On Friday November 22nd I was at home making a dress when I heard the news on the radio – President Kennedy had been shot in Dallas, Texas. Later we heard that he was dead. It didn't stop me going out the next day to see the Rolling Stones at Studio 51 in Soho. They were fantastic, as usual – when I was crammed in a basement with water pouring off the walls, sweat running down my face, jammed so tightly in the crowd I couldn't move my arms, I was at my happiest. Emerging, clammy and red-faced, into Charing Cross Road, I'd feel totally superior, part of the in-crowd, from a different world to the dreary people sitting opposite me on the Central Line from Tottenham Court Road out to the desert of suburbia. That's how it seemed to me, anyway. Now I could face another week of Miss Dyball and her bloody Latin O-level classes, my mother and her bloody nagging about my appearance, and my father and his constant moaning about me getting home late. Live music was what kept me sane and made me feel special.

8

Getting Started

A HOT AUGUST AFTERNOON. I'm standing on the first-floor landing of an artist's house perched on top of the moors in Cornwall between St Ives and Zennor. My bedroom has an imposing bay window with a 180-degree view across the moors to the west. Haile Selassie once slept here, when he'd fled Ethiopia – I wondered how Zennor compared to Addis Ababa. Even in summer this house is so exposed you can hear the wind all night long; maybe it reminded the deposed emperor of the desert. I'm bored, and I'm looking through a small window at a man sitting on top of a huge granite boulder in the garden directly outside. Hundreds of feet below, the sea is a brilliant turquoise and gulls swoop overhead. He has a

sketch pad on his lap, and with a soft thick pencil he's drawing the rock formations directly in front, turning them into a doomy mass of foreboding shapes. He's wearing jeans and a striped shirt, and his hair is thick and over his collar. For some reason, long forgotten, I am shouting at him, raising my voice above the breeze and the birds. I start to scream and gesticulate, pointing madly in his direction. I put my hand right through the glass and I don't care. He's just too infuriating for words. Why won't he do what I want and go for a walk . . . why does he insist on spending hours churning out these tormented drawings? Why is he such a misery in everything he does?

I spend the next day dozing fitfully in the emperor's bedroom, my head pounding. My first migraine, a symbolic moment in a doomed relationship. My troubled affair with Rex, spanning nearly three years, saw me change from gawky schoolgirl into college student. I told him I would marry him, and then finally I dumped him for someone I'd met only forty-eight hours earlier.

By 1964 I was combining a lot of A-level homework with going to jazz and blues clubs several nights a week, in Soho, Chelsea and Hampstead. I would go with a couple of girls from school or Joanie, my only friend on our dreary housing estate in Perivale. The Six Bells club, a large room over the pub in the King's Road, Chelsea, was held on Thursday and Saturday nights. Throughout this period it was one of my regular haunts, and I hardly missed a week, spending hours on the Underground or on buses in freezing weather travelling considerable distances to gigs.

Night after night I would sit on the wall at the back of the platform at North Acton station, and pull my leather jacket around myself against the freezing wind. One

Thursday at around 11.30 p.m. I was in my regular spot, praying that a West Ruislip train would arrive soon, and shivering – not because of the cold, but because I was already anticipating the all-too-familiar row when I walked through the front door. I'd had a great evening at the Six Bells club in Chelsea listening to the Alexis Korner Blues Band, and had even been bought a couple of beers by a cute mod boy (who sadly vaporised when it came to closing time), but getting home could take up to an hour and a half, and my curfew was 11 p.m. I'd already caught a bus to South Kensington station, got the Circle Line to Notting Hill Gate and changed on to a Central Line train, but had to change at North Acton and wait for one to West Ruislip. God, how I hated living in Perivale!

As far as I was concerned, Perivale was a cultural desert, a cul-de-sac off the A40 road out of London, and nothing more. The local pubs played country and western or Cliff Richard. If I wanted to hear decent live bands performing, like the Rolling Stones or Manfred Mann, I would have to be prepared to travel long distances. But I was a committed fan, and so it was all worth the effort. In my diaries I faithfully recorded what bands I saw along with what clothes I was making to wear.

I was seventeen, and looking suitably fashionable was all-important, and so I spent hours slaving over a sewing machine to get exactly the long narrow look that suited me. My skirts were long and narrow and covered my knees with kick pleats at the back, and I teamed them with square-toed shoes with high thick heels from Raoul, a shoe shop in Soho. I would make tailored over-blouses to go under my (by now acceptably aged) leather jacket. I made shift dresses that were cut in at the shoulder, skimmed the hips, had piped collars and pocket details. Handbags had to have long straps, your hair had to be sleek and chopped. It was a very precise look, and I spent a lot of time and effort working on my version of it. Perivale was a mod-free zone, where boys wore jeans and girls had little sense of style.

Top of the Pops had just started on television and in January the Rolling Stones had played their first tour as headliners — soon they'd be playing stadiums and they were leaving my club circuit behind. Now I'd travel to see hardcore blues bands like John Mayall who still played at small venues, and then save up to see visiting blues legends at the Marquee club like Sonny Boy Williamson. Through making friends with the guy who ran the record shop in the King's Road near my school, I'd been taken to see jazz greats like Duke Ellington and the Modern Jazz Quartet, who attracted a massive following of students and young people. But I had pretty wide tastes – the first single I'd bought was 'Carolina' by the Folks Brothers, on the BlueBeat label. I found it on a stall in the market in Shepherd's Bush by the Metropolitan underground line. This record, made in Jamaica, was a catchy reggae number, the kind of music you only heard in very few clubs in Notting Hill Gate or Soho at that time, and certainly not on the radio. Because it was such a cult, it became a mod anthem, its syncopated beat turned into a series of mod dance moves.

At seventeen I was desperate to lose my virginity. It seemed like a ball and chain, holding me back. I just needed to get it over and done with. I simply had no real interest in exploring sex, but it was something that needed to be ticked off, so I could move on. The previous year I'd failed to get Hugo, the boy I met on holiday with my parents, to do the deed. Thrillingly, they had decided to forgo the annual grim pilgrimage to Llanfairfechan and had saved up for our first (and my last) package deal holiday. We travelled from Luton airport and flew to Gerona, travelling by coach to Lloret on the Costa Brava – my first trip to Spain. Our hotel was a white concrete box and the food pretty basic, but in those days this part of the Costa Brava hadn't been over-developed and the town itself still retained some of the charm it must have had when it was just a fishing village. My parents soon settled into a routine of lying in the sun all day (Dad had gone an embarrassing shade of brick red), and spending the evenings after our dinner (included in the price so we never ate anywhere but our hotel) in a series of bars drinking with other English holiday-makers.

I had met Hugo on the beach on our second day there as I posed about in the waves (I'd never been swimming in warm water before!) in my fetching, white one-piece swimsuit. He was tall, thin and extremely studious, with short, dark-brown hair and a cute, small goatee beard. He

was at the Ecole Militaire in Paris, studying to be a bomber pilot in the air force. After a couple of nights in discos, we'd indulged in some heavy petting on the beach but, try as I might, I could not get Hugo to have sex with me. He was far too well brought up and sensitive, just my luck. My parents thought him charming and well-mannered, too well-mannered for my taste. After I came back to England he sent me a blue and white striped matelot T-shirt, like the one he'd worn on holiday, with a note saying it was best we didn't correspond any more as he wanted to concentrate on his studies. And so I was still a virgin, and very pleased when a cute black boy called Jimmy got

on the wall. I remember struggling to get my long tight skirt off, lying down on a narrow single bed, a bit of squidging about, momentary pain, and it was all over.

A foggy Sunday evening and I caught the bus back to Tottenham Court Road and the Central Line home. I was shaking with excitement, relieved I'd finally done 'it'. I had absolutely no interest in whether I saw Jimmy again or not. That five minutes in a grotty flat in north London was time well spent. The next day I went to visit my mother who was in hospital recovering from an operation on her over-active thyroid gland. She had a scar which stretched right around her neck. Shame they didn't chop her head off, I remember thinking. As I stood at the foot of the bed, her eyes narrowed. She could tell. I imagined it was because I walked differently. Perhaps the gap between my skinny thighs had widened, who knows. I felt unbelievably superior at school, not daring to tell any of my classmates, or even my best friend Liz. Our friendship was based on music, clothes, mod-dom, not on any form of intimate revelation. We had never once discussed our emotions.

I didn't bother with any form of contraception, and my diaries of these years have joyful circles around that date each month when I got my period. I even used to count out the days, 28 one month, a nerve-racking 31 the next. Before I'd even had my next period I met a very strange tall young man – probably about twenty-three to my seventeen – at the Six Bells one Saturday night. He had extremely thick messy long hair, a large nose, a rather plummy voice, and Joan and I dubbed him Boris – our way of marking him out as someone who didn't exactly fit into mod stereotype. He bought me a beer, and then another. We didn't dance, but stood together listening to the band for an hour or so. At the end of the evening he brought me home to Perivale on his scooter, and revealed his real name was Rex. In spite of trying to act cool I was actually quite impressed by him. In my working-class circle of friends I had never met anyone who had such a posh name, or who had been to private school. Rex also came from Surrey, a county I had endless fantasies about as it started where the Underground ended and we occasionally visited Leith Hill or Box Hill for picnics in the summer.

Rex seemed to embody this middle-class respectability I had perversely craved, coming from the kind of background I had imagined my fantasy parents might have had. He was working for the well-respected architectural firm of Yorke Rosenberg and Mardall in Holborn, during the gap year of his architectural degree course at Kingston College. It was certainly a step up from working-class youths with names like 'Nobby' who I had been pursuing at local clubs near my home. They were almost always trainee butchers or builders.

We went to the cinema in Tottenham Court Road a couple of days later, and when I got home to Perivale I wrote in my diary, 'I just don't know what to make of him.' I didn't have any point of reference about how to deal with someone like Rex, he was quite outside my limited experience with men. He was to be my first real boyfriend, and I could only tell my diary all my doubts and anxieties as I had no close female friend who I felt I could reveal my secret thoughts to. After school on Friday I left the Underground at Notting Hill Gate and caught the bus to Westbourne Grove, where Rex was renting a second-floor flat on Hereford Road. We played records, and indulged in some heavy petting. I liked the way he kissed, and he certainly wasn't sneery about my appearance or intellectual pretensions.

Home life was stormy, as usual. My mother was out of hospital and my parents were constantly on my back over my many late nights. They were concerned that I was not spending enough time studying for my A-levels. I had begun to realise, though, that exams were only part of how you got on in life. Through Rex I continued the process Eileen had started, soaking up movies and theatre, but now a new range of magazines and buildings as well. He was absolutely instrumental in showing me a wider range of possibilities, replacing Eileen as my mentor.

After I had endured a particularly turgid trip to the seaside with my parents – we drove to Worthing in the family car and sat huddled on a rug on the windswept beach eating gritty egg sandwiches from a tin while my father brewed tea with a primus stove – we had a tremendous row. I felt my father told my mother things about me behind my back, having endless opinions on my clothes, my makeup and my boyfriends, but didn't have the guts to say any of it to my face. He was thoroughly petty, not to mention pathetic, obviously desperate to meet Rex, but too grand to ask me to my face. I was going to make him wait.

I was seeing Rex three times a week, going to the Marquee, queuing to see the Modern Jazz Quartet in concert and the harrowing new play *Who's Afraid of Virginia Woolf*? The writer, Edward Albee, laid bare the antagonism between the two central characters (played by Liz Taylor and Richard Burton in the movie) and the ensuing rages and tirades were all too familiar. At 2 Bleasdale Avenue my parents fought all the time, interspersed with hours of sulky silences. I couldn't imagine a domestic existence where people had normal conversations and were genuinely interested in each other. My home was like a war zone, with my father constantly shouting orders at me: 'You're not going out looking like that! Clear up your room now. You WILL be back by 11 p.m. or ELSE!'

After Rex brought me home late after a blues concert, another screaming match ensued and my parents demanded to meet him. You could say that from the moment the three had tea together, all the real danger and excitement vanished from our affair. Mum and Dad were impressed with his middle-class manners, his posh voice, his qualifications. All worries about who was seeing their daughter three nights a week evaporated overnight. Rex was in a different league to the scruffy local boys I had been seeing at the local youth club. By now I had started sleeping with Rex at his flat in Notting Hill Gate, dropping off there on my way home from school, but it wasn't that memorable. I can't have been very knowledgeable about sex, and certainly can't remember having an orgasm. By May, less than two months after we'd met, Rex and I were bickering, especially when the ancient scooter he used to ferry me home late each night broke down. I met his extremely respectable middle-class parents, who seemed rather cold and formidable, and stayed the night in their house in Banstead, sneaking from my room to give Rex a wank in his bed in the middle of the night. That was both naughty and dangerous.

By the end of May I thought my feelings for Rex were changing. The initial excitement had worn off in some indefinable way. It was always good to see him, but I didn't miss him at all when we were apart. As mods and rockers rioted on the seafront in Brighton and Margate, I wondered about Rex. Sure, he was cleverer than the average working-class mod, but was he boring?

Meanwhile we went to the Tate Gallery to see the 54–64 show about contemporary art, in which I would see the work of the English pop painters like Joe Tilson and Richard Hamilton for the first time. I loved it. I was inspired and excited by music, art, new things, new experiences. My boredom threshold was extremely low, and I was already getting tired of Rex. I could hardly be bothered to talk to him on a date – I preferred to see a movie or go to a gallery.

Rex bought me 'Dimples' by John Lee Hooker, a track I adore to this day, but we continued to bicker. He got on my nerves because he never fought back, just sulkily tolerating me. I persuaded him to let me cut his hair by promising lots of sex, trying to mould him into something I would find more captivating. He was totally puritanical about his appearance, and extremely reluctant to accept any kind of remodelling.

I was enjoying a passionate embrace in a sports car with a man I'd met in a local club around 11.30 one night when to my shame my father strode out of our house in his dressing-gown, opened the car door and dragged me inside, screaming abuse at the man behind the wheel. Once in the hall he punched me and shook me fiercely, grounding me for the next couple of nights and instituting a 10 p.m. curfew. All to no avail – his daughter had well and truly left the coop mentally and physically, even if I still kept up the pretence of eating the odd meal there and sleeping in my single bed. My parents and I had nothing in common, no conversation, no small talk. They weren't interested in the films I was seeing, the art that inspired me, the plays I saw at the theatre. My dad's favourite topic of conversation was the state of the traffic on the A40, and all my mother ever asked of me was that I'd come home 'safely' and 'take care' whatever that meant. My relationship with Rex seemed cursed by their approval.

One night at the Marquee I was listening to the well-respected Joe Harriott Quintet, one of the really interesting new wave of modern jazz groups around at that time. In the break, Joe, who played alto sax, came up and asked if he could buy me a drink. We started talking – we'd seen each other at clubs several times before (the modern jazz scene was a pretty small world), and our friendship just gradually grew. I would go around alone to his ground-floor flat in Clifton Hill off Maida Vale after school and hang out while he rehearsed or played records. Sometimes other jazz musicians would be there, playing cards or smoking. I'd just drink tea and chill out. Joe would call me a couple of times a week, and we'd go for a drink and play bar billiards in his local, or I'd go and see him play at the Bull's Head in Barnes. Sometimes he'd cook me supper. We would occasionally hold hands, but that was it. He just liked seeing lanky Janet sprawled across his sofa. Rex knew about Joe, and was deeply suspicious.

In July I met a good-looking Greek student in his early twenties called Minas at a party in Kensington that I had gone to with Rex, and secretly pocketed his phone number. I found his curly dark hair and chiselled features very attractive. Next day we played tennis in Battersea Park and the day after I went to his room near the Science Museum where we made love. Minas seemed very active and energetic – it was a bit like shagging the PE teacher. He also reprimanded me about my posture, saying I should not slouch. He showed me the exercises he did every morning, which had given him an impressively rock-hard stomach. I feebly tried to emulate his militant style.

Back in the semi-detached world of Perivale, my mother had a huge row with Dad and stormed off for a few days. Neither my sister nor I had any idea what had caused this latest major eruption. My father certainly wasn't going to tell us, and slammed the front door as he went off to his allotment and probably the pub for a few hours. I was bewildered. I couldn't imagine either of my parents having an affair – the very thought of them participating in sex made me feel queasy. I could only imagine it was a row over money or where to go on holiday. We made our own meals, my father acted as if nothing untoward had happened and we enjoyed several days of blissful peace and quiet until she returned on July 10th, her birthday. My sister and I greeted her return as if she'd just popped down to the parade of shops at the entrance to our estate to buy a bag of sugar. She offered no explanation. As usual this incident was never mentioned again.

I continued to see Rex, and especially enjoyed going out with his friends Royce and Rhoda. Royce was studying furniture design at Kingston and they lived in Hampshire. Royce and Rhoda were friendly, easy-going, middle-class people, and I loved Royce's ironic sense of humour. They both were a lot of fun to be with, much lighter company than Rex, who always tended to be introspective and morose when by himself. We saw Ray Charles in concert at Hammersmith, and went to Rex's office summer party which was held on a boat sailing up the Thames with Sandy Brown's band playing, a brilliant evening at the height of summer. The next week I saw Lindsay Anderson's *Lord of the Flies* at the cinema in Upper Regent Street, and the scenes when the fat boy was bullied gave me nightmares for days afterwards.

By August Liz and I had decided to go on holiday to Belgium for two weeks, which my parents had reluctantly sanctioned, while Rex and his friend John were planning a trip to Denmark and Sweden to stay with friends. Rex was a compulsive letter writer and not a week passed without an envelope arriving at Bleasdale Avenue with his familiar scrawly handwriting – he always used a Rapidograph, the pen architects used to draw with. Over a two-year period he must have written to me at least fifty times, and in this, the early months of our courtship, they were signed 'yours', with kisses, but they soon became more demonstrative, ending with lines of kisses and incorporating sketches and doodles, often of himself looking miserable. In our complicated relationship I frequently created unpleasant scenes and found Rex guilty of non-existent crimes. In the very beginning, I may have been slightly intimidated by this well-read, cultured older man, but within five months I had reduced him to a neurotic wreck who was constantly writing letters of apology.

Part of my Machiavellian way of operating was to

persuade Rex that I would miss him madly. Consequently he wrote to me every single day for the month he was travelling, recounting every aspect of his trip to Denmark and Sweden, taking in Copenhagen and Stockholm. It seemed to rain a lot and he got bitten by ferocious mosquitoes.

This was the first time I'd been on holiday without a chaperone, and I planned to make the most of it. Having flown from Southend to Ostend, Liz and I took the bus to Blankenberge, staying in a modest hotel a couple of streets back from the seafront. And what did we do? Went to clubs every night, dancing, rarely getting to bed before 1 a.m., meeting up with some cheery teenage mod boys from north London called Ben, Ray and Steve who were staying in our hotel for breakfast each morning for a full debrief about the previous evening's activities – what clubs we'd been to, what people were wearing, what records got played. On my return, I found a bundle of letters from Rex waiting for me in Perivale. Secretly I had found my own holiday boring, and wondered what Rex was getting up to. He'd been to see the Beatles film in Stockholm and was planning a trip to a jazz club. I couldn't bear the idea of him having more fun than me. But by now his cards revealed he was fretting over the lack of decent nightlife, fed up with Scandinavian food – a diet of smoked fish – and running out of money. Rex wrote to tell me that his father had given him a loan for the holiday, and had remarked that I would no longer be interested in him when he was a penniless student. This was hardly true, as even when he was working Rex had little money left after he'd paid his rent. If he had been able to earn money, surely he'd have swapped his ancient scooter for a more reliable form of transport. His lack of money didn't really bother me anyway; I had initially been attracted to him because of his middle-class background. Now Rex had packed up the flat in Notting Hill and would be returning to college in Kingston for the final two years of his course in the autumn. He wasn't sure that he could afford a flat.

With Rex still away, I enjoyed a week or so of freedom before he returned, and I secretly met up with Hennie, the Dutchman who had been his flatmate in Notting Hill Gate. Hennie was another of my clandestine male acquaintances, someone I would meet occasionally and even tell Rex about in order to make him more jealous.

romantic jazz score to the film *Black Orpheus* made a huge impression on me – it seemed to express some secret longing I could not yet articulate. Meanwhile, I still cultivated back-burner men. At a party in Surbiton I met John Russell, another Kingston architectural student, hiding his phone number for future use. We secretly met for dinner in Richmond the following week, and it galvanised the suspicious Rex into buying me flowers and writing a passionate letter. He knew I was up to something, but couldn't work out what. He seemed anxious he might be losing me, and my outrageous behaviour seemed to mark a new phase in our relationship.

By December the pirate station Radio London was broadcasting and Parliament voted to abolish the death penalty. I would listen to the radio in my bedroom night after night, while I struggled with my homework. I tried not seeing Rex for a week, but we soon resumed our tortured affair. Rex wrote from his parents' house: 'I'm sorry we have had a couple of quarrels. I wanted to kick you up the arse, but I expect you felt the same. They were either directly my fault, or worse, me not understanding.

Next term when I have a room, we will be able to be more physical in our fights, which will be better as they will pass sooner – and you hit harder than I do . . .' We were conducting a relationship surrounded by parents, in small suburban rooms which were too hot or too cold, and sex was difficult. We were both stubborn and single-minded. He was a depressive and seemed to be a masochist for submitting to my torture. He also promised not to be jealous when I was chatted up by strangers at parties. (He should have been more suspicious, perhaps.)

On Christmas Eve Rex stayed the night at our house, sleeping on the sofa. He gave me seven gifts: rings, drawing books, paperbacks and a scarf, and I presented him with a pair of slippers. He made me a card seven feet long – it seemed to sum up our lopsided relationship. Christmas came and went, and both of us were fighting with our parents. Rex's rows were all over money – his parents would not give him any kind of loan. He still did not have enough funds to rent a flat, and we spent the festive season shuttling between Perivale and Banstead, cooped up in claustrophobic living rooms with irritating relatives. We escaped to Tod Browning's extraordinary film *Freaks*, set in a circus, with a whole range of physically challenged performers. I had nightmares for days afterwards, and wished I hadn't ever been tempted to see it. I spent the holidays working in Holland Park Tax Office once again and I saw that my mother was a changed person at work – with a different circle of friends she seemed lively and reinvigorated. She definitely enjoyed the camaraderie of office life, with all its petty intrigues. But too much had happened for us to be friends, and I took to sloping off on my own at lunchtimes.

Finally, I took Rex to meet Joe Harriott and we all played bar billiards at a pub in Maida Vale. A wary truce prevailed.

9

Good and Bad News

I PASSED THE BLONDE woman an envelope containing £25 in cash – she checked it carefully and put it in her apron pocket. 'Take your knickers off and sit on the edge of the table, please.' Numbly, I just did as I was told. My heart was beating frantically, and I was absolutely terrified. But I had no option, I had to carry on with this, the alternative was blowing my one and only chance of going to college. How could I have been so stupid as to get pregnant? As I lay back on the towels spread out on the table, I let my mind drift forwards to the exciting prospect of training to be an architect. I tried to ignore what was happening below my waist.

*

1965 had started with a dreary little party in my parents' front room in Perivale, celebrating — if that's the right word — with a couple of glasses of sweet sherry with Rex and my sister. I felt completely stifled by the people closest to me. I'd spent my eighteenth birthday at his parents' house in Banstead, and it was so cold I had cried at the bus stop on the journey back home. This year was going to mark another fatal stage in my relationship with Rex: over the next twelve months I would make the transition from school to college but spend every week fighting with the man who I now had firmly in my thrall. Later, for absolutely no reason whatsoever, I got engaged to him. I know this all sounds like the behaviour of a demented woman, but I honestly believed that the only way to escape the constant carping and criticism at home was to get married.

Rex was still looking for a flat, and we argued endlessly over my relationship with Joe Harriott, who I adored. Joe wanted nothing from me except companionship, and I found his flat a good place to hide in, listening to jazz and drinking beer. It wasn't even as if Joe and I ever had sex, but obviously Rex suspected we did. He was also still suspicious about my friendship with his former flatmate Hennie – in that instance, rightly so! In the autumn I had made the decision to study architecture and had applied to the Bartlett School at London University and the Architectural Association, down the road in Bloomsbury Square. In preparation for my interviews, I went to the Tate Gallery to see the exhibition of paintings from the Guggenheim Collection and toured the galleries on Bond Street. I spent a weekend photographing buildings in the city of London and Billingsgate fish market. I was gradually preparing myself for the tough selection process I would have to go through for college.

Another term started at Lady Margaret's and I felt locked into the tedious routine: endless commuting across London, doing homework, reading in my cluttered bedroom with the door firmly shut to keep out the family. I was a mass of contradictions, spending so much time with Rex's friends, people older than myself. I no longer considered myself a schoolgirl. I could hold my own in conversation, especially opinionated on everything to do with films, fashion and modern art, but I harboured enormous insecurities about how I would fare with my university applications. In those days, the

Architectural Association had university status, although it was an independent college. It had a tremendous international reputation, and was considered a hotbed of ideas, with lecturers and students from all over the world. My written application for admission was the result of hours of input from Rex and his college friends who considered themselves experts in filling in forms. I wrote: 'I feel that architecture is the field of design which is the most important − as it is part of our essential environment. It also seems to require the disciplines of logic and practicality, disciplines I feel I would respond well to.' What pretentious bollocks, in retrospect! Nobody from Lady Margaret's had ever studied to be an architect, and I was taking History of Architecture as one of my A-level art papers, preparing by myself in the first-floor library, reading about Renaissance Rome and the building of Florence. I took a final excursion to Canterbury to photograph the cathedral, sticking all my architectural photographs in a series of notebooks with captions.

The night before my entrance examination for the AA, Rex wrote me a little note of encouragement: 'The element of luck will be small and it will be in your favour . . . you should have the intelligence and skill to master the questions . . . any drawing required is a projection of your understanding of why things look the way they do. Don't panic, and don't be depressed either by the questions or your opinion of your own answers . . . all my love, Rex.' Joe phoned, wishing me luck too. The examination itself was held at 10.30 a.m. in a large vaulted hall in Queen Square, in Holborn, and lasted two hours. Row upon row of brown wooden desks had the exam paper laid face down when we filed into the room. It was a bitterly cold day, and there were about fifty boys and just one other girl. The questions were a mixture of the aesthetic and the practical, and I was deeply depressed, convinced I had done really badly. It seemed to me that some of my fellow applicants had an aura of confidence about them I simply didn't possess.

We spent the following weekend with Rex's friends Royce and Rhoda in Hampshire, and I tried not to think about what I'd written and drawn on those sheets of paper the Wednesday before. Next week, on the day my new, knitted, Mary Quant black mini dress was ruined at the dry cleaner's, I got a letter from the AA saying I had been successful in my examination and was now summoned for the next nerve-racking stage, an interview. I saw three foreign films in succession that week, including a Russian version of *Hamlet*. I was hoovering up input, often dreaming of events taking place in the landscapes I'd seen in the cinema. I would spend hours on the Central Line staring out of the window imagining the Russian steppes or a Parisian street – anything rather than the dowdy reality of North Acton with its humdrum industrial estates and scrap-metal yards. Because I had failed O-level Latin, I didn't even get as far as an interview with London University, and I was plunged into misery when the letter arrived with the bad news. I seemed to be spending my life in a daze, sitting in arthouse cinemas or standing in clubs listening to really loud music. I was treading water, waiting for a new set of friends, a life away from school, home and my suffocating parents.

My interview for the AA took place at the end of January 1965. By then I'd prepared a portfolio of drawings and photographs put together over the preceding couple of months, and I felt more confident. The experience of talking about what I was interested in and why I wanted to study there was an easier hurdle to overcome than the previous ordeal of the written examination – never my forte. I had Rex to thank for months of encouragement. We still had fights over the most inane things, and I stormed home from the cinema one night on the bus, only to foolishly answer the phone to him the next day, and when he apologised for being morose I agreed to see him again. The one thing I never did was say sorry, even when I had started a fight over some imagined shortcoming on his part.

A week later, I was sitting in an English lesson at school when I was summoned to the headmistress's study. Her secretary said there was an important phone call for me. It was Mum – she'd come home from work at lunchtime and opened a letter addressed to me. It was the fantastic news that I'd been accepted at the AA. Even in my moment of victory she had to interfere and deny me the thrill of finding out for myself. I was totally elated and finished the rest of the day's lessons in a dream – even when I got home from school I couldn't be bothered to complain about her outrageous behaviour in opening my post. There was too much to celebrate! More good news: Rex had finally found a flat to share with two college friends over the river from Hampton Court, in a detached Victorian villa in Palace Road, East Molesey. It was on the first floor and consisted of three large airy rooms and a kitchen. Perhaps now our relationship might be more harmonious as we would have somewhere private to meet, away from our families.

I received three Valentine cards, two from Rex and one postmarked Kilburn – could it have been from Joe? I never did find out.

I continued my weekly trips to the cinema, seeing *North by Northwest* and *Breakfast at Tiffany's* one after the other, and I adored Audrey Hepburn's clothes. I immediately started to work on a shift dress like the one she wore in the film, doctoring a pattern I'd bought in John Lewis when I went to an interview for the Central London Polytechnic School of Architecture in Regent Street. I had decided to go through with the application just in case I didn't get good enough A-levels for the AA. Sharpening up my image, now I was to be a student, I bought a new dress by Gerald McCann at Woollands department store (now Harvey Nichols) in Knightsbridge, false eyelashes, and new black lace-up shoes from Annello and Davide. To complete my new look, I ordered more flattering Oliver Goldsmith glasses. I was still making most of my clothes, spending hours hunched over a sewing machine.

At a party in Richmond one night with Rex, I encountered John Russell again, the architectural student from Liverpool I'd met the previous year. Mindful that Rex was shadowing me like a hawk, I whispered to John that I would be in contact.

To try and please me, Rex bought me a silver ring, but I had already secretly written a note to John Russell giving him my phone number. I was very pleased when he called and we arranged to meet while Rex was busy with a work project. John, meanwhile, posted me a detailed map of how to find his flat in Surbiton. Funnily enough, it was in exactly the same road as my art teacher at school — I hoped I wouldn't run into her. The next Saturday, I visited John and we made love for the first time on a mattress in the middle of the floor of his room. He was not exactly my physical type, for although he was tall he was too podgy for my taste. But he was from Liverpool, had a good sense of humour and just having sex with more than one person made me feel very desired and special.

In the run-up to my mock A-levels I didn't see anyone. Joe phoned half a dozen times, but I stayed in and revised. I couldn't afford to blow my chances of escape. I needed to make sure I passed at least three A-levels to be certain of a college place, and I found the Mathematics revision particularly difficult. I spent the next few weeks totally focused on work, not going to clubs or seeing anyone in the evenings. Exams over, I resumed seeing Rex, and didn't bother with any further contact with John Russell. Life was complicated enough without getting another man involved. I left him on the back burner, to be activated in the future if I got bored with Rex. Now Rex had moved into his own flat I helped him decorate it; we painted the room white and he put a mattress on the floor in the middle of it and a drawing board along the wall. I cooked him cauliflower cheese (the limit of my culinary expertise after being forced to give up studying Housecraft), and we spent Sunday mornings in bed before walking along the towpath by Hampton Court. We'd watch the ducks paddling in the shallows and laugh at the people chugging past in their dinky little cabin cruisers. I would pretend to my parents I was staying with his friends or his parents, constantly fearful they would be checking up on my alibis.

At times like this I hoped our relationship would enter a more harmonious phase now that we had a room to go

in except Rex. I simply could not afford for anyone to find out anything about my situation, let alone my parents. As we had never discussed sex at all, the idea of mentioning casually over breakfast that I was expecting a child seemed ludicrous. Apart from anything else, we didn't talk much at mealtimes, let alone about anything of an intimate or personal nature.

I stumbled through my A-levels in a daze. Through a friend we found out about a woman in Camden Town who would deal with the situation for £25 cash. I arranged to see her one Friday after school when my parents had gone away. Rex wrote to me in code: 'It would be of little use to be emotional at the moment – fear, despair, sadness will not help the situation. I must accept full responsibility and take most of the decisions on your behalf. I regret only that up to now I have lived such a sheltered life as a student . . . that what is expected naturally frightens me. Without being callous . . . we must remain unemotional, and regard what we must do as a series of tests or obstacles which we can easily surmount if we remain level headed. When it is over I think we shall even be happy, in a way, that it occurred, we shall be stronger, even closer. I will be stronger and more self-confident and better for you. Please be brave . . .'

I took the tube to Chalk Farm and walked up Malden Road, stopping on a corner to ring the bell to a flat above a shop. I had decided to go through what lay ahead alone. I certainly didn't want Rex to be there. A blonde woman let me in, took the cash and showed me into her kitchen. Shaking with fear, I took my knickers off and sat on a towel on her kitchen table, leaning back with my legs apart. She stuck a syringe of something (soapy water, I don't know) up me, seemed to scrape something around a bit, which was painful, and then told me to go home and I would have a miscarriage in an hour or so, just like a heavy period. I barely made it back on the Central Line to Perivale before the cramps started – they were terrible. I spent hours sitting on the lavatory losing a lot of blood. Luckily my parents and sister were away for the weekend. It was pretty disgusting, but all I felt was a tremendous sense of relief. Providing I hadn't totally fucked up my A-levels I would still be going to the AA in September.

On Wednesday 28th July 1965, my last day of school, I took my loathed Lady Margaret panama hat (I hadn't worn it in the sixth form), walked up to Putney Bridge, and threw it in the Thames. My school diploma noted that I had been a member of the 1st tennis team and the Art Club. I was also the School Charity Representative (a shameless move to get something worthy on my college applications as I had zero interest in charity or worthy causes). I'd never made it as a prefect or form captain, but I did have a good academic record, in spite of the recent abortion and potential A-level disaster. I couldn't

wait to go to college, and mix with a different group of people. Although I would stay in touch with a couple of girls for a couple of years, we were starting to grow apart. In the long term, I knew that I would never see any of my school friends again. I wanted to be successful and famous, not tied down by family, boyfriends and any kind of a routine. There was a single-minded ruthless streak to me which I recognised, and I knew I was starting on a long journey alone.

Before I started at college in the autumn I was going to have to earn some money and so I returned to my previous holiday job, in Holland Park Tax Office, for a couple of weeks, spending a lot of time secretly reading files instead of delivering the post. I would crouch in the storeroom where all the self-employed people's files were kept, looking up famous actors and actresses who were resident in the area. Even though I had signed the Official Secrets Act, I got a vicarious pleasure in noting how the famous had the same tax problems as the rest of us, and came up with all sorts of reasons why they hadn't paid their tax bills. My next holiday job was at Peter Robinson's department store at Oxford Circus, where I pretended I wanted to be a handbag buyer as the pay was slightly higher than for a basic shop assistant. I would spend hours dusting the merchandise and trying to look busy, fending off the rush on the first day of the sales. In another money-making

venture I made some slim cotton ties from printed jazzy material I found in a street market and sold them to Rex's friends, as well as in a couple of boutiques off Carnaby Street I'd discovered in my lunch hour from Peter Rob's.

I felt disconnected from Rex because of the abortion, although of course he wasn't the only one to blame. When I got my A-level results at the end of August I hadn't done as well as everyone had expected (not surprisingly), failing Pure Maths, getting a good grade in Art and reasonable ones in History and English – enough to ensure I could still attend the AA, however. My parents were extremely worried about the cost of me attending college – although my tuition fees were to be paid by Ealing Council, it was only prepared to give me a maintenance grant of £152 a year and expected my parents to contribute another £161 a year towards my upkeep. Of course I was never going to get any money out of them – according to Mum the £161 was the cost of my food. It meant that I would have to live at home and travel to the AA each day, more hours every week on the bloody Central Line. I felt as if my whole social life revolved around the times of the last trains out of Notting Hill Gate. When I received a letter from the Secretary of the AA listing the girls who would be in my year, in case I wished to share a flat with them, it just made me even more miserable.

At the end of the summer, before term started for both of us, Rex and I went to Paris for a week. It was my first trip to Paris and our first trip abroad together, and spending this much time in each other's company was a novel experience. I was entranced – we spent hours walking the length and breadth of the city, up to Montmartre, to the flea markets in Montreuil and Clignancourt, along the Seine, wandering through the back streets in St Germain, looking in boutiques, and visiting the Louvre and Musée des Arts Décoratifs. I collected postcards of all the sights that impressed me and started to stick them in a book.

When we returned we decided to get engaged. I had bullied Rex into asking me one evening by threatening to leave him if he didn't make some kind of commitment. Now I had had an abortion, this was an emotive issue, as I felt I had been through a horrible experience mostly caused by him. Rex, for his part, was really insecure that I would leave him for someone else – he repeated this time and time again in dozens of letters he sent me. I weighed things up and saw an engagement as a means of escape from my parents and the claustrophobia of life at home in Perivale. The fact neither of us had any money and I was just eighteen seemed totally irrelevant. Maybe Rex thought that if I started college with a ring on my finger I might be faithful. Fat chance. Anyway, both sets of parents seemed pleased, and we received good luck cards and presents from our friends. In my life I refer to this as wedding 1a, because, as things turned out, it was a completely false start. Rex bought me a Victorian moonstone and gold ring from Cameo Corner near the British Museum, which I proudly wore like a huge diamond trophy. We held a drinks party in the front room at my parents' house and I received three pop-up toasters and a set of cutlery as engagement presents. My rarely seen relatives in Wales and Manchester sent cards of congratulation. For my part, I certainly had no long-term plan to end up Mrs Rex Thomas, but I was keeping quiet on that score.

I O

A Swinging Student

A MAN WITH A huge mop of tightly curled hair and large heavy-framed glasses was looking at me sympathetically. 'Is there a problem?' he asked in a booming fruity voice. There certainly was. I'd been at my new college for less than five hours and I was about to fall at the first hurdle. We'd been asked to do a drawing of how a bicycle worked and I simply had no idea. I might as well have been asked to recite the Koran while standing on my head. I was a whiz at having an opinion about everything from the merits of the Beatles versus the Stones and the uniqueness of Richard Hamilton's Pop Art prints with their imagery of Marilyn Monroe and body builders to the wearability of the latest futuristic metallic clothing designed by Paco Rabanne. But asking me how anything as mundane as a bike actually worked presented me with a real problem. For a start I'd never actually been allowed to own one as a teenager. After a few accidents on a tricycle, roller skates and two-wheeler bikes were banned from the Bull household before I had a serious accident and any more ambulances might be called, causing my parents further embarrassment.

My first day at the Architectural Association was extra-ordinary. Ninety boys and about half a dozen girls milling about on the top floor of the college main building in two elegant Georgian houses at 34 and 36 Bedford Square in Bloomsbury. I quickly struck up a friendship with Piers Gough, an extremely extrovert, loud, jolly, tall man with a shock of frizzy hair. He sat immediately behind me. After he obligingly came up with a bike diagram I could pass off as my own, we went for a cup of tea and it marked the start of a friendship that has lasted to this day.

Most of the boys had attended public school and many were away from home for the very first time. They had no idea of how to cook or even dress. They were over-whelmingly middle-class and white. I felt far more sophisticated and worldly than most of them, primarily because I'd been hanging out with Rex and his friends for so long, and also because I knew Soho, the shops, cafes, pubs and clubs, like the back of my hand. From the age of fifteen I'd visited the place every week, whereas some of my fellow students were like ducks out of water. Within a couple of weeks Piers and I had a core group who we would hang out with in the bar and at lunchtimes, filling in each other's names in the register when we were late for lectures, and going to parties together: Paul Burrows, a beautiful boy with long dark hair; the quietly spoken, red-haired Rex Wilkinson; upper middle-class and quietly funny Philip Wagner; Keith Cowling, a working-class mod; a hilarious Jewish boy called Roger Zogolovich; and Mark Fisher, who we called 'the northerner', rarely seen without his trademark large baggy shapeless sweater. Another friend was one of the few girls, Katharine Heron, the eldest daughter of the distinguished painter Patrick. Katharine, because of all the people who had visited her father at home in their house at Zennor outside St Ives, seemed extremely cool for her age.

I plunged into college life, becoming engrossed with new friendships and caught up in the exciting change in the way I was taught. We went from classes about History of Architecture, studying Greek hill towns with Joseph Rykwert, to completely dull lectures on building materials taught by a dreary chap with the hilarious (to me anyway) name of Cecil Handisyde. He seemed to be obsessed with efflorescence, which turned out to be mineral deposits staining brickwork. One minute I was in a life-drawing class, the next swotting up on structural mechanics, always to be my weak point. I was so full of ideas about how I wanted a building to look, and so painfully unable to absorb all the practical information needed to make the ruddy things stand up. Soon we were designing our first project, a small shelter on Primrose Hill, and I had the first chance to realise my ideas in three dimensions.

As Christmas approached, we threw ourselves into preparations for the carnival, the big annual college party. It had a Prohibition theme and Piers and I were on the committee. We planned to flood the courtyard at the rear of the main buildings and construct a boardwalk out

of scaffolding around it. I was in my element, turning ideas I'd seen at the movies into sets for parties. These were really exciting times, and it's easy to see how my relationship with Rex began to suffer. I also was gradually shedding the few school friends that remained, caught up in a frenzy of parties, movies and college dances. We regularly went to gigs at the Royal College, St Martin's and Central art schools, and I remember seeing Jimi Hendrix playing live at Imperial College one unforgettable night in South Kensington. We'd just never encountered anyone who played the guitar with such dazzling ferocity, such showmanship, such effortless artistry. Hendrix made most blues and rock guitarists seem leaden and pedestrian in comparison. He moved the goalposts.

The AA hosted a lot of avant-garde art events, and the situationist Gustav Metzger caused a sensation when he set fire to a piano in the name of 'auto-destructive' art. Not surprisingly, the press were enraged – we of course thought it was a bold and subversive act in which art and politics were fused. London was a hotbed of ideas, and we had lectures from visionaries like Peter Cook of the Archigram Group, who produced a series of manifestos of their plans for the city of the future designed like brightly coloured comic books. In one, buildings had legs and moved like machines through the environment. Cutting-edge architects like Hans Hollein and Buckminster Fuller came to London to give lectures, adding to the feeling of excitement as radical new ideas were discussed and ideas exchanged. Bands like the Kinks had played at college dances and now entered the mainstream. The crossover between art, music and fashion was intense.

As my first college year progressed, I became very friendly with Peter Murray, a fourth-year student, who had devised an avant-garde magazine about architecture

called *Clip Kit*. For your subscription you got a plastic binder and a set of new pages each month. Peter shared a flat in St Edmund's Terrace, north of Regent's Park, with a bunch of friends including Johnny Goddard and Hilary Lane who were studying painting at the Slade, and I would frequently spend the night there, occasionally sleeping with Peter, who was really just a friend. Peter and I would take trips around the country selling *Clip Kit* at conferences and at other universities, something Rex wasn't too happy about.

By now I was designing and making startling clothes from silver PVC, skinny coats and trousers and miniskirts, and selling them to a shop off Carnaby Street called Palisades. A fellow student, Paddie Minns, made me perspex buttons shaped like dominoes for the coats, and we were both making quite a decent amount of money –

I no longer bothered with ties. My hair was long, and I cut quite a striking figure, sporting Bermuda shorts and a big fur coat I'd picked up in a flea market.

Piers and his friends were sharing a flat in Notting Hill Gate, so I had another bolt-hole away from the dreariness of Perivale. Nevertheless, I worked extremely hard during this first year at the AA — having nearly ruined everything with the abortion the summer before, I was determined to make a mark. My attitude to sex, however, was frankly totally childish. I was totally amoral. Being engaged meant bugger-all, the long-suffering Rex was just my fall-back position, someone I'd see when there was nothing else on offer. I remember that one of the students in our year was older than the rest of us. A charming, well-spoken, good-looking man in his early thirties, Nick had been through Sandhurst and served as an army officer. Some of the boys bet me I wouldn't sleep with him. In the end I took them on for about £5 in cash, and inveigled my way back to Nick's flat off Ladbroke Grove. I can remember very little about the experience, except for his freckly skin, which was a first, and I triumphantly produced a gas bill at college the next morning as evidence, in order to pick up my winnings.

Another time, at a party with friends from college, I decided to seduce Terry Farrell, now a hugely successful architect but in those days one of our lecturers. To win my bet I had to have sex with him and be back at the party within two hours, which I just about accomplished. At nineteen, sex was just a bit of sport with no emotional ties. I still used no form of contraception, because the Pill was not readily available, and we didn't always bother using condoms, because somehow it took the spontaneity out of the moment. Living at home meant that I still used the same doctor as my parents, and I couldn't risk them finding out about my sex life. I still marked each time my period started (with massive relief) in my diary, as I had done for years.

I bumped into John Russell by chance at a party in Chiswick in February – I hadn't seen him for ages. Now my life revolved around Bloomsbury and London's West End, rather than Kingston, although Peter Murray and I went down there one Saturday a couple of weeks later to sell his magazine. I went to an art opening with Katharine Heron and met her parents. Her mother, Delia, had been a distinguished potter, and was strikingly attractive and a lot of fun. Patrick Heron was eccentric and opinioned, and for the first time two middle-aged people talked to me as an equal, rather than an irritating schoolgirl. How I envied Katharine her parents – I had simply never met anyone like them, and they were to have an enormous effect on me. Soon I was having dinner with the Herons at their flat in Edith Grove in Chelsea, meeting artist friends of their generation like William Scott, Trevor Bell and Roger Hilton. Katharine and I went to supper with Eldred Evans, a young architect whose father was the Vorticist painter Merlyn Evans.

A new circle was opening up to me, and I went to stay with Patrick and Delia at their house in Zennor for Easter. Eagles Nest sat in the midst of an outcrop of enormous granite boulders high above the sea on the coast between St Ives and Land's End. The house had huge windows with wonderful views in all directions. We went to Newlyn and bought fish from the wholesalers, drank in the Tinners Arms in the tiny village of Zennor, and I photographed the crumbling mine chimneys on the cliffs at Pendeen, where we bought pasties in the village shop. I adored Cornwall – I hadn't been to this part of England since a summer in Mevagissey long ago. The conversations at breakfast ranged from tirades about art critics like Clement Greenberg to local gossip about the artist Roger Hilton's drinking binges. The Herons accepted all of Katharine's friends as part of their circle. I was in heaven.

My parents seemed small-minded dreary people who were satisfied with holidays in Spain and trips to the pub. You can call me a snob, and you'd be right, but I felt I had nothing in common with them whatsoever. We barely spoke, and I spent less and less time at 2 Bleasdale Avenue. It was only the lack of a full grant which kept me there. Back in London I continued to see the latest New Wave movies from the continent – Fellini's *Juliet of the Spirits* and Jean Luc Godard's *Alphaville*, with its bleak monochromatic vision of the future, the unforgettable female death squad carrying out their work in a swimming pool. I was thrilled to meet and talk to the visionary architect Buckminster Fuller (the man who realised all the potential of structures made from geodesic domes) after an inspiring lecture at the AA. Paddie Minns and I went skating and drank in Hennekey's pub on Portobello Road, a favourite hangout for the hip artists and designers.

Pop Art was really taking off in London, and I went to a party at David Hockney's flat in Powis Terrace, just down the road, where I met the artists John Hoyland, Peter Blake and Joe Tilson. Joe was one of the visiting lecturers at the AA, and before too long I was meeting him for drinks in pubs around Notting Hill and Greek suppers in small cafes off Charlotte Street in Fitzrovia. At thirty-seven, he was way older than me, and came from a working-class background. Harold Wilson was Prime Minister, but Joe's politics were further to the left. He was extremely well-read, self-educated really, with a thorough knowledge of philosophy and the classics. He spent a large part of each year in Italy and spoke Italian fluently. Joe's work was full of references to Che Guevara, Ho Chi Minh and the war in Vietnam, where the number of Americans killed was escalating. For him, art and politics were inextricably linked. Joe was also married with small children, a fact I chose to ignore. As far as I was concerned, we were just friends. Joe was lecturing at Oxford and I sneaked off to join him in a hotel for the night, losing an earring in the process. Joe wrote to me in Cornwall to tell me he'd just finished presenting a television programme about Leger ('never again – TV is hard work') and enclosed a lot of cut-out

AA. I failed my Structures examination, but was given a glowing report by my year master, and a pass to the start of the second year. He wrote: 'She could either make astonishing progress with brilliant results or deteriorate to the point of personal disillusion, which I believe will be a shame to herself and a loss to architecture.' Prophetic words – he'd already picked up on my lack of concentration, my inability to see a project through to the end. I also lacked confidence – not surprising when you consider my background and lack of support at home. I also found my friends like Piers exuded an energy that I found hard to match. He seemed equally at ease with the practical side of the course, whereas I was basically only interested in design, and lacked the application to consider the practical requirements of my 'visionary' concepts. To me, architecture was an extension of print-making, dress-making or fabric design – I was primarily concerned with the look of my ideas, rather than the humdrum (to me) business of making it actually function.

Meanwhile, my parents, who had been totally suspicious of Joe (who'd taken to dropping me back at their house after our suppers and drinks in his distinctive silver Land Rover), had their worst fears realised one night when we turned on the television in time to see a report on the Venice Biennale, and there was Mr Tilson, with Mrs Tilson on his arm. Another screaming fight, and I retreated to my room, plotting escape. Now I can see how hypocritical all this was – when Mum and Dad first met, they were married to other people, who they thought nothing of cheating on. The very idea of my parents berating me for having an affair with a married man, for actually dating more than one man at once! To me they presented a carefully contrived image of moral rectitude. I was supposed to be saving myself for Rex (ha, ha!), and my wedding, whenever that was going to be. My mother announced that I made her 'feel ashamed', a constant refrain in the years to come. I once thought of having it embroidered on a bloody needlepoint cushion for her sofa, she'd shouted it at me so many times.

In a determined effort to force me to focus all my attention on my career, my father, who was now working for the London Borough of Brent as an electrical engineer in their offices in Wembley High Road, northwest London, pulled a few strings to get me temporary holiday work as an architectural assistant for the princely sum of £11 a week. The job was to last a month, and it already seemed like a prison sentence to me as he would be driving me to and from the office each day to make sure I got there on time. I was soon a total embarrassment to Dad, however, turning up for work clad in a silver PVC miniskirt with huge silver hooped earrings. On day one they asked if I was the new secretary, and when I replied that I was the new architectural assistant they looked distraught. I was put to work on a new sports centre, and soon abandoned the idea of constructing anything as dreary as a building. I devised three inflatable domes, with all the changing rooms underground – very cutting edge. I was emulating my heroes at Archigram, and the work of Cedric Price. I embellished my drawings with comic strip characters, much to the chagrin of my team leader. It was the summer of the football World Cup, and travel in and out of the office was a nightmare. We could see Wembley Stadium from the office windows and the high street was packed with fans. My father meant well, but I loathed the whole experience, the canteen lunches and hours of tedium. Surely there were more fun ways of earning money – but I knew that it was a condition of college that I put in the time in an architect's office.

At the start of the summer break, Piers threw a party at his flat in Notting Hill. I went with Peter Murray, and was irritated that Rex turned up. We were technically engaged, but hardly seeing each other. His friends were so much more serious than mine. Attending a dreadful party given by one of them, I wrote in my diary afterwards, 'Boring night, loads of architectural discussions, I just feel like an intelligent accessory.' Meanwhile, I was so involved with Peter Murray – who was secretive, smart, and hard to pin down – that I wrote to him, 'file me under interests – current! I think this is going to be the best summer ever, don't you? Haven't the last few weeks been great – I will never forget them. When I try to recall other affairs, this one is too happy and sad and beautiful to tell you. Predictions are pointless. Read this how you like!'

I got an order for over £70 to design and make coats from a boutique in Carnaby Street, and spent my evenings running them up so I'd have money for a holiday. I wasn't very amused when a man came up to me at Oxford Circus and intoned, 'I . . .AM . . .A . . . DALEK' before bursting into hysterical laughter. I thought I looked totally chic in my silver plastic mac and matching miniskirt.

I'd written to Katharine Heron, and planned to spend the rest of the summer down in Cornwall, as her parents were going away on a lecture tour in Norway. We would have the house to ourselves and could really throw some parties. 'Are you bringing a beau?' she wrote to me. 'And if so, which one?' On August 6th, I caught the train from Paddington alone – now the fun could begin! Katharine and her sister Susanna and I went immediately to the Tinners Arms in Zennor and the evening degenerated from there. The following morning we went to St Ives to sunbathe on beautiful sandy Porthmeor beach. The weather was fantastic and I did a bit of babysitting in the evenings to earn more cash, as well as sewing coats for Palisades during the day on a battered old sewing machine in the small front room off the hall in Eagles Nest, where Patrick used to paint watercolours.

A week later Rex arrived with his friends Tim and Chris, and thirteen of us sat down to supper in the cosy bar of the Tinners, after which we had a party at Eagles Nest. We ate mackerel we'd caught off Treen beach and went to the Minack outdoor theatre on the cliff top at Porthcurno to see *The Tiger at the Gate* by Girardoux. I found it interminable and fell asleep, lulled by the crashing of the waves on the rocks below. Rex was a bit of a wet blanket, I couldn't imagine why I'd asked him as we argued all the time and it meant I couldn't score with any of the gorgeous men we were encountering in local pubs and at the surfing championships at Sennen Cove. After one particularly fractious morning I screamed at him through the window on the first-floor landing of the house. I stabbed my finger at him and put my hand straight through the glass. I hardly noticed, he enraged me so much. My mother wrote to tell me a friend of Joe Harriott's had introduced himself when he was working in her office (she was then in a tax office in Harlesden) and that Rex had been on the phone to her the minute I left London 'with all his little tales of woe'. Even my long-suffering parents were perhaps beginning to realise that this man was extremely depressing.

Back in London, Peter Murray had got a job on *Nova*,

the new stylish women's magazine where Molly Parkin was fashion editor and Harri Peccinotti the art director. From the graphics to the photography, *Nova* broke all the rules. Its photographers, from Just Jaekin to Jean-Loup Sieff, created fashion imagery that made *Vogue* and *Queen* look frumpy in comparison. Molly created fashion spreads of beads, furs, details shot in extreme close-up. I loved it, and Peter and I became friends with her. Meanwhile Rex's friends Kit and Sheila got married in Aylesbury – I could feel the noose tightening. Rex's letters to me around this time were all about cash and the lack of it. He just seemed so miserable and hard done by. I, on the other hand, floated from party to party, saw Joe Harriott again, and planned a trip up to Liverpool to see John Russell before I returned to start my second year at the AA. John was working in his gap year from Kingston in Liverpool City Council's architect's department. I arranged to go and stay with him for a week at the end of August and go to the TT races on the Isle of Man.

My first impressions of the Liver Building and the docks were tremendous. The area hadn't yet been restored into the trendy flats and shopping centre they are today. I marvelled at the scale of it all, the curved stones on the quayside, the sense of space and light, the interplay with the water. We visited Liverpool's massive Anglican cathedral and the extraordinary Catholic one (nicknamed Paddie's wigwam by the locals) designed by Frederick Gibberd whose son was one of my friends in the first year at the AA.

I wasn't that interested in John Russell physically, and I slept in the small spare bedroom at his parents' house on a council estate on the outskirts of the city. We went to clubs and pubs and a raucous wedding reception and I loved the atmosphere, the ruthless cutting wit, the rowdiness of it all. We took the late-night ferry to Douglas, cuddling up to keep warm, and arriving at daybreak. I remember the neatness of the island, travelling on a restored Victorian train, while John photographed and sketched me. My interest in motorcycle racing was minimal, and all I can recall is standing at a bend for a couple of hours enduring the endless screeching and swerving and trying to look suitably cool and enthusiastic.

On my return to London, John Russell sent me some

photographs and a poem about our time together. It was clear to me that he had a romantic vision of me that in no way could I live up to. In some ways it scared me, and it put me off contacting him again. I needed to find a way to be friends rather than lovers with him, but I was not old enough or sophisticated enough to work out how to do this. Emotional ties were not my forte.

II

Wedding 1A Bites the Dust

IT WAS 9 O'CLOCK in the morning and I'd been up since 6.30, crawling out of a mattress on the floor at a friend's flat in north London, pulling on red and yellow striped PVC trousers, sticking on false eyelashes, outlining each eye with thick black pencil, squinting in the mirror propped up on the mantelpiece. Next, a quick spray of silver on my long matted hair, pulling on a tight vest. My outfit completed by a silver plastic coat. Half a cup of black instant coffee (ugh!), then a dab of white lipstick. In St Edmund's Terrace the only sign of life was a milkman, who looked incredulous at the sight of me folding myself into the front of a small van with a couple of equally flamboyantly dressed men. Soon we were speeding out through the suburbs of north London to the studios at Borehamwood, praying that we weren't required to do very much before we could have breakfast.

I didn't think that filming would be this much hard work. On arrival we were shepherded into a large studio where about a hundred other people were listlessly sitting on a few chairs or lying on the floor. A couple of Equity officials were sitting behind a trestle table, and we were asked to form an orderly queue to register our names and addresses to qualify for temporary membership – £5 would be deducted each day from our wages. By now we were frankly mutinous, desperate for coffee, a bun, a bacon sandwich, anything. Suddenly a hush descended: Signor Antonioni had entered our holding pen. He walked up and down, looking carefully at everyone, followed by a whole retinue of self-important-looking men and women with clipboards and walkie-talkies. When he reached me, he smiled and asked me to wait on one side. Soon afterwards he picked out a tall, good-looking black guy. Everyone else was herded into the next studio, where our scene was to be shot. For the next hour, he meticulously arranged everyone in position, and gave them a mark.

I was placed in a gap with the black guy, and told that when the band started playing I had to dance. 'Why did he pick HER?' hissed one of the professional extras in a stage whisper, who clearly had the hump because the regular crowd fillers were far outnumbered by this motley band of students that the director had encountered in bars, colleges and clubs around Soho. Everyone else was told to remain as still as possible. My first moment of fame – albeit in a non-speaking role! After forty-five minutes, wasn't enough room in the main building of the AA for all the students in my year, so about ten of us managed to get selected to sit in a basement studio on the other side of Bedford Square at number 6a. We discovered that the Imperial Hotel on nearby Russell Square was going to be demolished. A vast Edwardian structure with Turkish baths, nightclubs and hundreds of rooms, it was full of junk we could incorporate into our new surroundings. Four of us went round to the back entrance where stuff was being loaded into removal vans by teams of men in cream overalls. We nicked four of the coats from an office and soon were our very own removal team. Soon 6a Bedford Square boasted bentwood coat stands, a leather sofa, and numerous hotel artefacts. I got dozens of pairs of white towelling slippers from the Turkish baths and some huge meat plates. Our new studio had its own payphone, another plus. Not being part of the main college premises suited us down to the ground as we did not want to be under too much surveillance from the staff – we all intended to combine studying with as much paid work as we could get away with. Piers and I had business cards printed with the payphone number on them. I was still reminiscing on the part of the adults. I crawled into a single bed early. Thankfully we left at noon the next day for the dreary journey back down to London. I was not to see my cousins ever again, much to my mother's disgust.

Early in October I met the Italian film director Antonioni in the bar at the AA – he was looking for students to be in a film he was shooting in London called *Blowup*. A charming, quietly spoken, middle-aged man, he had a limited command of English, but through an assistant he asked Piers and me to an audition at the Porchester Baths in Bayswater – we were to wear our own clothes. In the end a whole gang of us got taken on. The only trouble was we would have to report for work out at Borehamwood at some ungodly hour of the morning. The scene being shot was set in a nightclub, with the Yardbirds playing. David Hemmings, the star of the movie, came into the club as the band were smashing up their instruments. It was a piece of cake. We would have to pay a small sum of money to Equity each day to become temporary members, but all the job involved was a lot of standing around looking cool – no problem there, then. And, to make it even better, I adored the Yardbirds and was totally besotted with Jeff Beck. With any luck I might even get to meet him! In my PVC trousers and silver plastic coat I certainly cut an outlandish figure – think of a Dalek played by a string bean and you've got the look.

The highlight of the filming was the arrival of the tea trolley at about 10 a.m. each day. Suddenly hordes of starving students would stream out of the studio and besiege the poor tea lady, who fled in terror. David Hemmings was stuck up, as far as we were concerned, not deigning to talk to us. With hindsight I know he was terrified – this was his first big film part – and I later read that he was sleeping in the Rolls-Royce he drives around in the film. As a group of people we thought we were super-trendy and weren't at all grateful to be chosen. In our eyes we were doing Mr Antonioni a bit of a favour by giving his pathetic movie a touch of credibility.

In that scene I can spot so many of my friends today – Manolo Blahnik the shoe designer, who'd just come to London to work in an antique shop, Piers, and loads of people from college, Paul Burrows, Philip Wagner. I got extra (£35 a day) 'action' money for my bit of dancing, much to everyone's disgust. In the summer holiday Peter Murray was working as a location finder and assistant art director on some other Italian films that were being shot in London. Directors were flocking to exploit the 'swinging' scene. In one, directed by Tinto Brass, I played a receptionist in a beauty salon in South Kensington. I wore a white nylon overall that barely covered my backside, my spectacles were removed and Mr Brass issued orders by waving white bits of card to show me where to go. In the backwash area of the salon, all the clients inexplicably wore papier mâché horses' heads. In another scene shot in an art gallery off Bond Street, naked couples simulated sex frozen like statues. My other scene starred Claudia Cardinale, and I had to lead her around the Turkish baths (now pulled down) in Jermyn Street, through hundreds of naked men and women. She wore a towel and I clung to my white overall, avoiding over-excited technicians who kept trying to push me in the freezing cold plunge pool once the sequence was in the can.

Of course all this social activity in our secondary careers meant that our time at college had to be even more focused. This second year meant a lot more practical work and one of the first projects was to redesign Cannon Street Station, which Piers amusingly did by coming up with a building shaped like the word 'trains'. My effort was thought to be somewhat confused, but as we progressed to the second stage of the project we seemed to be able to produce something slightly more coherent. I was secretary to the film society and also the representative for BASA – the British Architectural Students Association. Plunging into the minutiae of college life, I soon whipped off a letter to BASA saying the AA would be resigning unless they produced detailed accounts.

My college notebooks contain sketches for dresses I planned to make, interspersed with circulation plans for Cannon Street concourse! John Russell wrote, begging me to visit him in Liverpool, where he was still working in an architect's office, and I cruelly said I would be coming in October to an architectural conference – with Rex. My day-to-day existence in London was still a mixture of movies, clubs, pubs and parties. My favourite place to drink was the Salisbury in St Martin's Lane with its beautiful ornate mirrored interior, or the raucous Prince of Wales in Portland Road in Holland Park. For budget dining we regularly went to Jimmy's Greek restaurant in a basement in Soho, where you got vast plates of moussaka and doorstops of thick white bread for virtually nothing. Every day a group of us from college would lunch at the same working-men's cafe, Fiori's, in Hanway Place around the corner from Tottenham Court Road. With a decor unchanged since the 1950s – all brown wooden panelling and Formica – the menu featured hearty platters of stuffed heart, kidneys and casserole of oxtail, but somehow I could never stomach this proletarian fare. Perhaps it reminded me too much of growing up in Fulham, and the pie and mash shop in North End Road.

On our trip to Liverpool, Rex and I stayed with a friend of John's and ate in Chinatown, drank at Casey's and went to Paddie's market. John, not surprisingly, seemed rather depressed. On my return to London I grilled Rex over lunch and discovered that he'd seen someone during the summer – behind my back. To be honest I didn't really care but, being a totally self-centred dominatrix, I enjoyed making him suffer. As he studied for his finals I went to a party in Battersea with Peter Murray and Hilary Lane, and we let fireworks off on Battersea Bridge on Bonfire Night. Now, planning the AA's Christmas carnival for the second year running was taking up plenty of my time and I made lists of all the materials needed to transform the cafe into a Wild West environment.

The end of November came and went, and I hadn't had a period for six weeks, but I was so busy with my social scene that I hardly noticed. Gradually I realised I had to do something about it and I took to running up and down the escalators at Tottenham Court Road underground station and drinking vast amounts of cheap red wine, but nothing happened. John Russell wrote regularly with news of all the friends I had met in Liverpool, but now he tactfully sent regards to Rex, and had toned down the romantic content, adopting a self-deprecatory tone instead. Finally, at the end of November, I presented my Cannon Street scheme to the 'jury' of tutors, and to my astonishment they managed to like it.

*

Tim Street-Porter was in his final year at the Regent Street Polytechnic. He'd spent a year living and working as an architectural assistant in Berkeley, California, in 1965, and had become friendly with the San Francisco-based rock groups Country Joe and the Fish and Big Brother and the Holding Company. Tim had been making 8mm cine films of Las Vegas and Reno, and had put together a show of these together with his slides of graphic imagery from the West Coast. Someone on the carnival committee thought it would be great to invite him to screen them on one of the walls during the evening. The following Saturday I went to the theatre to see *The Bedsitting Room* and to supper with Rex. I started throwing up really badly (I'd taken some quinine pills suggested by a friend in order to bring on a miscarriage), but still my period hadn't started.

The following Thursday, Rex and I went to see Tim's films at the ICA. The evening was called *Captain America* and I was really impressed at the combination of trippy rock and three screens side by side showing multiple imagery simultaneously, changing in time to the music. Tim was friendly with some of Pink Floyd, and knew Roger Waters through college – later we would hang out

And so Tim and I met and had supper with a couple of his friends, a dress designer and her boyfriend, who was in Tim's year at college. They were good company, older than me, middle-class and pretty sophisticated. I got in late and lied to my parents about who I had been with. On Saturday morning Rex telephoned and we had a furious row. I refused to see him and skipped off to meet Tim in Earls Court. We drove over to have lunch with the Street-Porter parents in Blackheath near Greenwich in south-east London. They lived in an impressive Georgian detached villa with a blue plaque on the front announcing 'Nathaniel Hawthorne worked here', just off the heath, a bleak and windy expanse of grass high above Greenwich, with views over London for miles around. Tim's mother Marjorie was a miner's daughter from the north of England, who had come to London looking for work in the 1930s. She got a job in a florist's shop in Sloane Street, Chelsea, which is where she met his father. Marjorie had eradicated all traces of her working-class accent, however, and was a formidable character. Tim's father, Cecil, came from a family of landowners in Suffolk who had lost their large house and all their land in the 1920s. He was an idea where to start. I picked at the artichoke, watching how they took theirs apart. Dissecting the pheasant wasn't too bad, although I was mortified when I nearly broke a tooth on a piece of shot!

Tim's sister Rosalind was about my age, and studying at Bristol University — I liked her a lot, she seemed very lively and a lot of fun. I returned to Perivale not revealing where I'd been. On Sunday Tim and I went to a movie and afterwards he took me to see his flat in Earls Court, where he shared a couple of floors of a big house in Penywern Road with four other people. I got back to Perivale extremely late and had one of the worst rows yet with my parents. Rex had been telephoning for me, and they had no idea where I was or who I was with. In the screaming that followed I told them I had no intention of marrying Rex, and I'd be leaving home as soon as possible. Where I went was my business, not theirs.

They were livid that I had decided to call off my engagement and my mother came out with the classic phrase: 'I can't hold my head up when I walk down the street, you are a disgrace to our family.' What utter rubbish. I crept out to a phone box to telephone Rex and told him

I needed to see him urgently the next day. We met at a horrible pub just down the road from my lunchtime caff in Hanway Place, called the Blue Posts. That lunchtime the tiny smoky bar was packed with drinkers. Rex looked white and drained, as if he knew what was coming. Above the din, I announced in a pretty loud voice, 'I'm sorry, it's all off.' When Rex, understandably asked, 'What?' I just said, 'Us,' and walked out, leaving the poor fellow behind. I felt a huge sense of exhilaration – bugger the wedding planned for the following spring, the engagement presents, the prospect of becoming Mrs Rex Thomas. All I wanted was Tim Street-Porter, stammer, slender hips, the lot. It felt as if a load of baggage had dropped from my shoulders. I almost danced back to college and the afternoon's lectures, trembling with excitement at the prospect of seeing Tim again. I had been totally swept off my feet by a man I'd just met.

Over the following weeks our affair was intense. A few days later I went to the AA carnival, with Tim; Rex was already being airbrushed out of my life. I didn't even bother going home that night, staying at Tim's flat in Earl's Court. He and I went to Portobello Road looking for Christmas presents, visited his parents again, and I stayed the night there. On Christmas Eve Tim dropped me at my auntie Vi's house (she had now moved out of Fulham to New Malden), as I had worked out this was a safer place to spend Christmas than the battle zone at Bleasdale Avenue. My Uncle Ray was an extremely ebullient character, and we all got along fine until my parents arrived at 5 p.m., when my mother started harassing me once more about calling off the engage-

ment. I returned home to Perivale in sullen silence.

On December 27th, my twentieth birthday, Tim came to tea, and my parents met him for the first time. It was a stilted occasion, but I hoped that now they would see how very nice he was and stop their recriminations over wedding 1A. The day was some-what overshadowed by the news that an oil rig had collapsed in the North Sea and thirteen people had been killed.

In all the excitement of meeting Tim and finally severing my relationship with Rex, I had neglected to deal with my most pressing problem, that of my preg-nancy. Now I took a deep breath and telephoned Rex. He would have to pay for it, I regarded it as his fault. I wanted a fresh start with Tim, whatever it took. Through a girlfriend I had been given the telephone number of a doctor in Kensington who might be able to help me. Dr Blitz's surgery was in a large Edwardian stucco mansion off Queensway, near Paddington station. He examined me and told me I was three months pregnant; I could have a termination but I would have to see a psychiatrist in Harley Street (a formality in those days, as termina-tions were performed only on psychiatric or medical grounds), making an appointment for a few days later. This time around I would have to have the termination done in a clinic — go to a nursing home near Epping Forest, have a general anaesthetic and stay there for at least four hours after the operation. I went to see the shrink, got his letter, and a couple of days later Tim drove me across London to a row of large detached 1930s brick villas where London blends into Essex, a place I had never been to before. The drive, through Stratford Broadway and up Leyton High Road, took place in silence. I was shaking with fear.

For some reason I was mostly frightened that someone might see me and tell my mother – God knows why. To this day I don't know anyone who lives in that part of London. I went into a bare, sparsely furnished, cream-painted room with a couple of metal-framed beds, undressed and put on a backless surgical gown. After handing over an envelope with £250 in cash and being given an injection, I slid into a deep sleep, and awoke a couple of hours later to discover a large wodge of sanitary towel wedged between my legs. I drank a cup of tea and was still feeling extremely groggy when Tim picked me up an hour later. When we got to his room at the top of the house in Penywern Road, I fell into bed and slept for hours, just dashing to the bathroom on the landing every couple of hours to change my pads. My sense of relief was huge, but it was tempered with a worry that I might have damaged my body by having two abortions in two years. I knew one thing – I wasn't going to get pregnant again. Dr Blitz had given me a prescription for the contraceptive pill, and I planned to take those little white tablets every evening without fail.

Next day, I returned to Perivale and kept myself to myself. Rex had taken to writing me sad letters, enclosing tickets for presents he had deposited at left luggage offices around London. I would go and collect them and bring them back to Penywern Road, opening them on the kitchen table. The first box, left at Oxford Circus, contained a wooden box of earth. The second, left at Euston, hundreds of white balloons. The third, left at Victoria, boxes and boxes of matches. Finally I picked up one in which a single glass flask of distilled water emerged from the protective packing. Then the penny dropped – my former fiancé had sent me the four elements – earth, air, fire and water – to signify his love. I couldn't cope with this tidal wave of passion, it made me feel extremely uncomfortable. Deep down I did feel guilty that I couldn't love him and had transferred all my passions and enthusiasm to someone else, but it couldn't be altered. 'Do not feel sorry for me,' Rex wrote, but I did. He didn't want my pity, but that was all I could muster.

On a cold wet Friday evening in January, just before the new college term started, my mother was standing at the washing machine in the kitchen pushing clothes into it. She started whingeing on about things in general, my late nights, my habit of calling in late to say I wouldn't be coming home, the appalling way I'd treated the faithful Rex, the burden I imposed financially on her, my lack of assistance around the house, etc. It was like a steady drone, and I can hear it to this day. My father and sister were out, there was just the two of us in the house. I looked at her and suddenly I had the strength to do it.

'SHUT THE FUCK UP!' I screamed. 'THAT'S IT – I REALLY AM GOING THIS TIME – I CAN'T STAND BEING WITH YOU ONE FUCKING MINUTE LONGER, YOU MISERABLE OLD COW.' And with that, I grabbed my bag and coat, turned on my heel and walked out, slamming the door behind me. My last image of her was a red-faced angry woman in an apron, with a cigarette lit in an ashtray behind her, open-mouthed in shock.

I almost ran to the station – as if she might follow, grab me and stop me – all the way along the badly lit path by the playing field, between the chain-link fences, over the road and into the station. I had absolutely no money on me whatsoever. I rang Tim and reversed the charges from a payphone by the ticket office. A train pulled in, and I ran up the stairs and just made it, breathless with the exhilaration and adrenaline of the last five minutes. My head was spinning, and I passed the twenty minutes to Notting Hill Gate in a daze. I changed and caught a District Line train, something I had done so many times in the past en route to Lady Margaret's School in Parsons Green. This time the journey was different. I got off at Earl's Court and walked purposefully up the steps, my heart beating. At the barrier I said to the ticket inspector, 'I'm really sorry, but I forgot my purse. Can I give you my address and send the money?' He nodded, and I said, '35 Penywern Road, SW5.' I wasn't going home any more.

List of Illustrations